WHO KILLED THE JINGLE?

STEVE KARMEN

HAL•LEONARD®
CORPORATION

Who Killed the Jingle?: How a Unique American Art Form Disappeared
Copyright © 2005 Steve Karmen.

Published by Hal Leonard Corporation
7777 Bluemound Road
P.O. Box 13819
Milwaukee, WI 53213

Trade Book Division Editorial Offices
151 West 46th Street, 8th Floor
New York, NY 10036

Library of Congress Cataloging-in-Publication Data
Karmen, Steve.
  Who killed the jingle? : how a unique American art form disappeared / by Steve Karmen.— 1st ed.
      p. cm.
   ISBN 0-634-06656-0
1. Popular music—United States—Writing and publishing. 2. Jingles (Advertising songs)—History and criticism. 3. Radio advertising. 4. Television advertising. I. Title.
MT67.K361 2004
782.05—dc22

                              2004014933

Printed in the United States of America
First Edition
Visit Hal Leonard online at **www.halleonard.com**

"PEOPLE DON'T HUM THE ANNOUNCER"®

is the registered trademark
of Steve Karmen.

A JINGLE IS ADVERTISING IN ITS
MOST MEMORABLE FORM:
MUSIC AND LYRICS.

NO SPOKEN WORD,
NO VISUAL IMAGE,
COMMUNICATES WITH THE
INSTANT RECOGNITION
OF A CATCHY JINGLE.

To Sandy, who only lived to see the beginning,
but inspired so much of the rest

To Lisa, Abbe, and Carrie, who became
my anchor and grew up to my music

To Savannah, Sean, Henry, Alex, and Audrey,
so that one day they will know the saga
of their magical Grandpa

To Peter Kelley, the genius who created my deal
and changed my life

To Nancy, who helped pick up the pieces
and make it all whole again

My love for each of you is endless.

Acknowledgments

I wish to extend heartfelt appreciation to these dear friends and respected colleagues who graciously shared their time and expertise with me during the writing process.

Morty Ashkinos, Lou Bellofatto, Mike Boris, Georg Bissen, Linda Bres, Peter Cofield, Keith Crane, Nick DiMinno, Bonnie Dolan, Bernie Drayton, Larry Geismer, Christoph Goebel, Lyle Greenfield, Vicki Gross, Alfred Hochstrasser, David Horowitz, Jan Horowitz, Thai Jason, Joey Levine, Jesse Levy, David MacMurray, Shaheen Motia, Danny Murtaugh, Hunter Murtaugh, Neal Platt, Ed Rak, Tony Rodriguez, Roger Rhodes, Jeff Rosner, Elliot Schrager, Paul Schulman, Jim Todd, Karl Westman, and Ginger Witt.

I am equally indebted to those colleagues who requested not to be identified for fear of reprisals.

Special thanks to Chuck Balis, Kenny Karen, Ken Olshan, Roberta Scheff Maneker, and Geoffrey Wharton whose honesty, keen eyes, and constructive commentary eased me through the rough spots that every writer endures.

Belinda Yong, my editor at Hal Leonard Publishing, won my gratitude and admiration for the energy, caring, and deep professional concern she added to each level of manuscript development that this work passed through.

Nancy Coyne never failed to provide encouragement and support. Nancy now knows more about the jingle business than any single individual ever needs to know.

Table of Contents

Introduction

In 1989, I wrote *Through the Jingle Jungle*, about how the advertising music business worked. During that process I interviewed people from all corners of the industry to learn what went on from perspectives other than my own. I sought a common denominator that might guide a newcomer through the inevitable minefields as well as provide some common sense choices that could help a professional who had hit a rough spot in a negotiation with an ad agency.

When I was asked to revisit the world of musical advertising for this book, to bring things up to date—a kind of before-and-after look—I was thrilled. I had enjoyed a great career and this would be an opportunity to learn about how the business has changed, and to write about it from the point of view of what it takes to make a living in advertising music today.

Again, I covered all the bases, interviewing stubborn holdovers from my era whom I hadn't seen in a long time, as well as music-house owners and their composer/arranger employees from the new generation. I listened to independent producers who worked in their home/office/garage studios; I visited ad agencies, questioning the music directors who gave out the work and the business managers who sent out the contracts; I spoke with film editors, musicians, singers, people who handled payrolls . . . anyone who was in anyway connected with the money-making mechanism of musical advertising.

Invariably, I left each interview stunned.

So many colleagues began with, "You can't quote me." An instinctive, but telling, response.

The flourishing industry that had once provided a substantial income for many talented people is no longer recognizable. Technology and poor business judgment changed everything. More than ever, the music supplier remains the doormat of the advertising community, and the *good old days* (my days) are looked back on by everyone as a kind of Madison Avenue "Camelot."

Is there an industry out there? Certainly. There's more advertising broadcast today than ever before. And more of it uses music, in one form or another, than ever before.

But who's getting the work?

And who's keeping the money?

And what kinds of deals are being made?

And why is there so little self-esteem in the ad-music business?

The answers I received, plus some reflections on the highs and lows of my own career—the events that formed my own personal way of doing business—make up the substance of this book.

The story, as it developed, was still about choices—the willingness (or not) to take risks and live with their consequences; and certainly about the vast differences between the way the industry worked then and the way it does now. But, more than anything, it became about the sobering reality of how difficult it is to stay in the advertising music business today, regardless of which era you came from.

As Don Corleone said to Don Barzini: "How did things get so far . . . I don't know . . . "

client, they'll still have a chance to make a pitch for their Heavenly Fried Chicken account.

All this political correctness usually leaves me feeling a little cheated. No one ever tells the story about the arrogant, pain-in-the-ass product representative who made the location shoot a living hell for everyone, and then fired his ad agency because his baby-sitter didn't like the commercials; or the self-serving account supervisor who caused a lost family weekend by insisting that everyone be ready for the big presentation by Monday at 9 AM, and then neglected to call everyone when the client informed him that he was golfing and wouldn't be showing up until Thursday; or the majestic agency business manager, in her one moment to exercise pure control, who purposely delayed processing the production invoice until she had been called and cajoled by the supplier at least three times, even though the supplier had already paid the talent within the fifteen-day time period required by the union. You know, the real stuff that goes on in the trenches.

The tone of what follows will be a little different. I'd like you to understand the mindset of the person writing this book.

I have always been self-employed. With the exception of two jobs I had when I was a kid—a soda-jerk in my senior year in high school, and a bookstamper at the public library for a month after I dropped out of college in my freshman year to go on the road as an entertainer—I've been flying on my own. That's my complete curriculum vitae.

I'm a self-taught composer and arranger, and during a twenty-five-year career in the advertising business I wrote a ton of music, primarily *jingles*—an unacceptable word at this moment—but also background underscores. I produced all my own sessions and, after I learned the ropes, insisted on working only on my own original compositions, refusing to rearrange someone else's music, turning those jobs down. I also held out to own my copyrights and publish my music—

Chapter One

The Mindset of the Author

Most books about the advertising business are written by agency owners, CEOs, and management types— past or present—who describe their journeys with a calm, respectful smile. No one ever says anything bad about anyone. Every sponsor ("the client") is a terrific person representing a terrific company that makes a terrific product, deserving pages of glowing praise and genuflecting for their endless benevolence. Ad-agency employees are portrayed as jolly little cogs in the big wheel of sell, existing only to keep their clients happy and to provide brilliant ideas for commercials. Outside suppliers (vendors)—music houses, film directors, video editors, sound engineers—if mentioned at all, are faceless footnotes who merely serve and obey, and (hopefully) bring their part of the job in on budget. Advertising authors always leave the door open so on that glorious day when they enter the big Madison Avenue–in-the-sky and meet a former

unheard of in the advertising industry—and to use my own contract form, which made for some interesting adventures on the far side of the keyboard.

I've never had the luxury—or burden, depending on your point of view—of a business partner to bounce ideas off; someone with whom I could share the work load; someone to raise a glass with when we won an account, or someone to Monday-quarterback with when we didn't get the job.

There was never a *we*.

It was always *I*.

Steve is a one-man show.

There have been others on my payroll—assistants, bookkeepers, accountants, song pluggers, music contractors, vocal contractors, lawyers (ugh, but sometimes necessary)—but I've always been the only creative type bringing in the business.

Still, to this day.

I worked in the comfort of my own home, then went to a state-of-the-art recording studio two or three times a week, where I spent a few hours with the best musicians and singers in town, who brought my music to life. My clients mostly left me alone to do what they had hired me to do. We ate a good on-the-job lunch, and when I came home there was money in the mailbox.

Sometimes there was no money in the mailbox. One of the "fringe benefits" of self-employment.

I truly loved doing it and I'm proud of my music. I like to think it represents a history of American business during a particular era.

I was honored to be elected three times as chairman of the now-defunct jingle industry trade association, the Society of Advertising Music Producers, Arrangers and Composers (SAMPAC).

The walls of my studio are decorated with slogans, catchy phrases, and illustrations that I find helpful in times of creative darkness and business uncertainty—inspirations for the self-employed.

Here is my top-ten of the moment, in no particular order, with author credits where available.

"YOU GOTTA HAVE POWER AND APPEAL IN YOUR VOICE. YOU GOTTA LET THE HOGS KNOW YOU GOT SOMETHING FOR THEM."
—Fred R. Paisley, Champion Hog Caller

"SOCRATES WENT AROUND GIVING PEOPLE A LOT OF GOOD ADVICE. THEY POISONED HIM."
—California sixth grader

"NEVER LET A DOMESTIC QUARREL RUIN A DAY'S WRITING. IF YOU CAN'T START THE NEXT DAY FRESH, GET RID OF YOUR WIFE."
—Mario Puzo, author of *The Godfather*

"NOTHING IS IMPOSSIBLE FOR THE PERSON WHO DOESN'T HAVE TO DO IT."

"A MAN MAY MAKE MANY MISTAKES, BUT HE ISN'T A FAILURE UNTIL HE STARTS BLAMING SOMEONE ELSE."

"WHEN THE OUTGO EXCEEDS THE INCOME, THE UPKEEP IS THE DOWNFALL."

"A CAMEL IS A HORSE DESIGNED BY A COMMITTEE."

"COPYRIGHTS DON'T TALK BACK."

"A DEADLINE IS THE ULTIMATE INSPIRATION."

"THE CEMETERIES ARE FILLED WITH IRREPLACE-ABLE PEOPLE."

That last one is for the campaign I thought would run forever, and didn't; for the residuals I believed would never stop, that did; and for the jobs that I was sure I had won that were awarded to someone else. Fortunately, there weren't too many of those—just enough to still sting after all the years. "Failure is the only true teacher," I've often said when lecturing about the jingle world. I remember the failures, and every one taught its own lesson.

There's a cartoon on my bathroom wall—a great place for inspiration—of five trees, four of them leaning away from a fierce wind, the fifth upright in the storm. The caption is: "Bend, you fool!" Sometimes I stood tall in the wind; sometimes I was blown away. The risks of the self-employed.

There's also a sketch behind my desk of a knight—a little guy I'm particularly fond of—coming home from what was clearly not a good day at the jousts. His hollow eyes have a beaten look. He's got a crooked cigarette butt dangling from one corner of his mouth, his armor is dented, his helmet askew, his lance snapped off at the handle, his shield dragging on the ground behind him. The caption says: "Some days the dragon wins." The hard-earned wisdom of the self-employed.

I've been involved in lawsuits; most were frivolous ego-driven wastes of money, and one major decision that became a landmark in the music business.

I have been incredibly lucky, instinctively brave when it counted, unbudgably tenacious when I thought the deal was unfair, and scared silly when I had time to catch my breath and wonder why my bulldozer bravado had so often replaced the common sense of giving in once in a while. The curse of the self-employed.

I learned early on that there is no such thing as loyalty in the advertising business; that the well-intended promises of people at the agency level were only as valid as the mercurial whim of their client; and that the good working relationship I had nurtured and counted on could disappear in a heartbeat when that individual took a better job somewhere else. This reality had a career-long impact on how I approached each contract negotiation.

I got along well with agency creative types—copywriters, art directors, idea people—but not so well with their business affairs managers and lawyers. When I found out that there were no rules out there for composers, I made up my own as I went along until I had developed a formula that worked for me. I took the rewards when I did well, and bore the heat when I didn't.

Most of all, I never lost sight of the fact that my agency client had entrusted me with a huge budget, approved by *his* client, and that they both deserved the best effort I was capable of giving.

I've always tried to maintain a sense of humor.

But some days, the dragon won.

Chapter Two

But *First*, a Little Then and Now

History and accepted lore have it that the jingle revolution began on December 24, 1928, on a local radio broadcast in Minnesota, when "Have You Tried Wheaties?" was performed for the first time. Advertisers had discovered a new and unique way of delivering their messages, with little songs that the public could hum and recall when they were not listening to the radio. Jingles told the whole story about the product with custom-made lyrics, and were recognized as new tools for mind stimulation. Soon, they were accepted as the foundation upon which to build a successful, long-term advertising image.

Let's imagine how it might have worked way back then, when the Chiquita Banana Company came to their advertising agency for help.

The account supervisor, leading the agency creative meeting, has just returned from a lengthy briefing with the brand manager of Chiquita. On the conference-room table in front of each person are a bunch of bananas and a strategy paper outlining the problems.

"I'll sum it up, boys: people are just not buying curved fruit. This year *round* is in. Look at apples. Look at plums. Skyrocketing! *Round!* That's what people want. People perceive curved as passé. Look at pears—in a nosedive. Look at pineapples—they have that warty thick-skin problem. We need to do something great for *curved* fruit, something unique and *edgy* to make the public aware of the benefits of bananas!"

The creative director: "Okay, let's examine the good things about bananas."

Copywriter One: "They taste great."

Copywriter Two: "They're less filling."

"Taste great!"

"Less filling!"

The creative director: "No, that approach doesn't seem right for this product category. Besides, apples and plums are doing taste campaigns, and we don't have the budget to outclout them. We've got to develop something unique. Let's tackle the storage problem. I think there's a different direction here—nobody is talking about fruit storage. Research shows that the consumer is concerned that bananas spoil quickly. What can we say about that?"

"Keep them in the refrigerator."

"Bananas don't do well in the cold, dummy!"

"Neither do I, Norman."

"I've got it! Instead of telling people about how a banana *tastes*, suppose we design a campaign about how to make bananas *last longer* when you get them home."

The account supervisor: "Sounds like a good start!"

Copywriter One: "I can write something about the art of ripening—that really sounds good, doesn't it? *The Art of Ripening*—with a warning not to put them in the frig. That'll make good copy. And it'll please the legal department; they like commercials with warnings. And let's use *music*. People love music. How about something *African*—bananas sound African, don't they? Let's get some African library music. It won't cost much. Native drums! I can write scary copy warning people not to put their bananas in the refrigerator."

The creative director: "No, we need something *friendly*, and something more distinctive than library music. We have to sound different, with our *own* sound that's not like anyone else's."

"Wait! Let's do it with . . . *a jingle*. That's right—with a *jingle!* I'll build the sets, you get the band and . . . "

"And I'll write the words."

"And let's invent a character to be the spokesman for the product. We can call her . . . *Chiquita Banana!* We'll make her look like Carmen Miranda—her turban can be made out of bananas—and *she* can sing our jingle!"

The account supervisor: "That's great, guys, just great! Keep it up! Does Henry-in-accounting still play the piano? See if you can work something up with him. But keep the costs down, okay? We're not apples and plums yet!"

This dialogue is hypothetical, of course, though not unrealistic. In the old *old* days, jingles like the great Chiquita Banana song were usually created from within the agency infrastructure—certainly the lyrics, and probably the music, too, which would have been composed by someone whose payment for the job was nothing more than his regular salary. (Henry-in-accounting did, however, get to lead the sing-along at the Christmas party.) It was the style then for things to be done *in*-house, since in the beginning there was no *out*-of-house. Later, as more advertisers began to use music to color the mood of their messages, independent companies started to pop up—*jingle houses*— that specialized in creating custom-made words, music and background scores specifically designed for advertising.

A business was born!

Fast forward. Cut to now.

An *ideation* session has just concluded at Uf-Tzuris, Worldwide, the global advertising agency conglomerate that represents "Zippy Sneakers." At the meeting, the copy department presented the creative and account team with a sixty-seven-page printout of all the pop-song lyrics found under the heading of *feet* at YourCampaignEasy.com, one of the websites used by the ad industry to identify music in every possible product category that is available for commercials.

Bob, the agency producer, has been instructed to contact several music houses to move this project to its next level. He dials his favorite supplier, Magical Music, one of the hot, new cutting-edge music production companies.

"Jim? It's Bob. We're developing ideas for 'Zippy.'"

Jim, the music house partner: "Great!"

"We'd like to hear some rough thinking by tomorrow night."

"Great!"

"We don't have a lot of money."

"Great!"

"Is Marvin available?"

"He's in China, on his honeymoon He didn't know this would happen. I'll page him. He'll come back tonight."

"Marvin's got a feel for cowbells. We're starting to hear cowbells. I'll e-mail you the strategy paper and a rough story board."

"Great!"

"We're not locked in to anything, but Harold wants everyone to look at 'I Have the Urge to Scratch Your Belt Buckle.' Remember the third reunion tour of the 'Bellbottoms?'"

"Sure."

"It's on their *Live in the Congo* CD. The sixth cut. The nine-minute version with the five-minute guitar jam. Harold likes the bass part under the piano and cowbell section about three minutes in. Anyway, it's a place to start. It's gotta work in thirty seconds, with enough room for twenty-five seconds of voice-over copy; and in a fifteen-second spot, with twelve seconds of VO."

Jim: "Great!"

"The other houses are sending in five different directions. Can you do that too? You know Harold."

"Sure. No problem."

"If you can get it here by noon, I'll try to get everyone to listen to your stuff first."

"Great!"

(Please note that the agency producer did not suggest, nor did the music house even dare ask, if the client would consider having *original* music and lyrics for his campaign. Nor did anyone broach the subject of whether the agency business affairs department had contacted the music publisher of "I Have the Urge to Scratch Your Belt Buckle" before ordering the demos; or spoken with representatives of the Bellbottoms or their record label about using the group's very expensive *Live in the Congo* actual recording. Let's not go down that messy legal path quite yet.)

Fortunately, Marvin does not have to leave his bride waiting in Shanghai while he flies home to supervise the demos. He calls one of his Asian colleagues from the Yin-Yang-Yingle House, someone he'd met at an industry seminar entitled "The Underrated Impact of Background Music and Sound Design in Effective and Memorable Product Marketing," and borrows their facilities for a day to oversee the production long-distance. Yin-Yang's small studio is situated on top of a chicken coop in a mudhut just outside of town, but Marvin is not concerned about sound-leakage: Yin-Yang uses Pro-Tools, the computer industry standard for digital recording, and all the music sounds will be created with electronic synthesizers. In case there is a need for live recording, the roosters know that any loud cackles will land them in the stir-fry, so Yin-Yang is as modern and cutting-edge as Marvin's own studio back home.

Jim e-mails Marvin the nineteen different first-idea demos that his New York composers have quickly put together; along with the Bellbottoms' recording of "I Have the Urge to Scratch Your Belt Buckle."

Marvin is a lucky man: while he was busy downloading, commenting, tweaking, and uploading tracks back and forth with the gang in New York, Marvin's young wife—a dutiful and understanding supporter of his crazy career, who was Marvin's sister's au pair when they met, and also sings on Magical Music's tracks when they needs a girl vocalist—has shopped in a local flea market and found several tiny oriental gongs that might work instead of cowbells. Marvin does a little computer magic, makes digital samples of the gongs, adds them to all the demos of the bass part under the piano and cowbell section about three minutes in on the sixth cut of the Bellbottoms' "I Have the Urge to Scratch Your Belt Buckle," from their *Live in the Congo* CD, now edited down to work in thirty seconds, and he and Jim decide together which five tracks to send to the agency.

The demos are submitted on time.

The Zippy client reviews thirty-five separate pieces of music e-mailed in from production houses literally around the world, and a decision is made: Magical Music's third demo is the winner!

The good news is that Marvin's honeymoon trip has now become an officially deductible business expense (it probably was going to be treated that way on his company books, any-way—you know, *researching new sounds*); the bad news is that demo-love is about to become demo-hell.

The agency producer calls: "Jim? It's Bob. Everybody loves the track, but we're still negotiating with the manager of the Bellbottoms, and just in case it doesn't work out, the client wants to hear a few alternatives. We'd like a version sung by a boy, and one by a girl, and one with both of them . . . "

"How about a vocal group?" Jim asks hopefully (everyone at Magical Music wants to qualify for the big bucks of vocal residuals).

"No, a solo or duo is better for our target audience, ages fourteen to fourteen-and-a-third."

(Damn, there go the residuals! Well, maybe Jim can talk Bob into letting four of Magical Music's employees shout, "Zippy Sneakers!" at the very end of the spot, which will achieve the same financial effect.)

By the time Marvin returns from his honeymoon, Jim has revised, restructured, resung, and remixed the track e-mailed in from the Yin-Yang-Yingle House. The sampled gongs are now more prominent than ever. In fact, the track has become gong sounds accompanied by a song.

The negotiations with the Bellbottoms, however, are not going well. As a backup position, Bob asks: "How much would it cost to rerecord everything with a huge orchestra, and travel to Romania to use the Transylvania Symphony, which works non-union, with no residuals?"

Marvin prepares a budget.

Jim books tentative travel arrangements.

At the last minute, the Big Three give in: the Bellbottoms' record label agrees to allow their *Live in the Congo* recording to be used; the Bellbottoms' manager agrees to allow the group's performance to be used; and the music publisher of "I Have the Urge to Scratch Your Belt Buckle" agrees to allow its song to be used.

The total cost to Zippy Sneakers? Almost a million dollars

for a twelve-month exclusive license in the footwear-below-the-anklebone category only. "But it's going to be worth it," everyone says.

It's time for invoices. Magical Music is instructed to bill the agency for a rearranging fee of $2,500 (even though they didn't actually rearrange anything, only edit the record and add the oriental gongs to the Bellbottoms' track), plus $3,750 to cover fifteen hours of studio time at $250/hour, even though it took almost eighty hours to complete all the revisions.

Bob, the agency producer: "We're really on a tight budget here, guys. We'll make it up to you next time."

Jim and Marvin, in unison: "Great!"

Finally, a few weeks later, the standard agency music contract arrives in the mail, a fait accompli, within which Marvin and Jim will sign away, forever, all rights to anything they contributed to the commercial, even the ownership of Marvin's new wife's little gongs.

Of course, included in the contract is an unlimited indemnification clause that places Magical Music first in line of jeopardy in case someone makes a claim against the track in the commercial.

The result of all this? Unfortunately, the agency copywriter provided too many words and the Zippy client wouldn't let them be edited, so the only lyric from the Bellbottoms' song that made it into the final version was "I Have the Urge . . . ," which was heard in the clear at the beginning of the spot and again in the fade-out ending, but this time covered up by a rapid-fire announcer, saying, "Open Friday night, free parking, bring the kids, toys and balloons for everyone, void where prohibited, member FDIC . . . "

The upside was that, because of all the quick-cut visuals of kids dressed in spacesuits wearing Zippy sneakers while playing paddleball on top of the Statue of Liberty's torch, America could immediately identify the product in the commercial as . . . their favorite mouthwash? Or was it that new deodorant that works for both you and your dog? Or was it for that laxative that also treats erectile dysfunction—*they made it work on both ends!* Or was it for . . . gee, I can't remember . . .

Hey, what's the difference? Was it good for you? At least you thought of the song, and it reminded you of your high school prom. What does it matter if you couldn't remember the name of the product? Everyone made a lot of money, right?

Well, almost everyone.

As one agency business manager said: "Yes, what the world definitely needs now is another light beer."

Chapter 3

There Used to Be a Business Here

"NEW IS AN OLD WORD. GET ME A NEW ONE!"
—Client to account supervisor

Mel Brooks's hilarious comedy character, the *2000 Year Old Man*, is a source of infinite wisdom on many subjects. When asked what the main means of transportation was two thousand years ago, he answers: "Fear!"

No word better describes the prime motivational force in the musical advertising business today.

At the outset, please allow me to define "jingle." This all-inclusive, easily recognized word describes an advertiser's audio image; a short custom-made melody with original lyrics about a product specifically designed to catch and hold a consumer's attention. Advertising music is not supposed to sound like other kinds of music: its job is to make the commercial stand apart from the program it is placed in, and to make sure the sponsor's message doesn't get lost in the non-stop barrage of ads that fill our lives each day.

"I write jingles," I would say when asked what I did for a living. I was working in a highly visible, high-profile art form, and everyone immediately knew what I was talking about.

"I think the commercials are better than the programs," would be the usual upbeat viewer critique, followed by, "I'll bet you make a lot of money, right?" And, "How can my kid get to sing on a jingle?"

That was then.

Today, custom-made advertising music has dropped off the radar screen and the effectiveness of the ads suffers accordingly. Now, the most-often heard consumer comment is, "There are too many commercials, and they're *crap* [à la Raymond's father]. You can't tell what they're for anyway; everything is noise with no melody, or songs that have nothing to do with the product."

The public has lost interest, no one asks about income, and parents would rather have their kids appear on *American Idol*.

I know I'm 180 degrees from current thinking, but it just doesn't make sense that an advertiser will invest close to a million dollars to buy thirty seconds of airtime on network TV, and then allow his ad agency to do everything possible to avoid sounding or appearing like they were selling something.

The phrase "cutting-edge" (or "edgy") came up again and again in every interview for this book. It's the industry buzz word, the ongoing metaphor for that elusive quality that every sponsor wants—"hip music with a smile in it," one composer delicately called it—something that is totally replaceable on a moments notice as soon as someone anoints a newer, though not necessarily more memorable, version of cutting-edge.

The advertising industry is often accused of being a business of imitation. If a special visual effect is developed for a motion picture—the flying people in *Crouching Tiger, Hidden Dragon*, for example—within a few months that same effect is certain to appear in a commercial for dog food. At one time, however, someone who worked on the musical side of advertising was considered a craftsman. The need to sound different was inherent in the job: it takes a special discipline to create a song that has a beginning, middle, and end, all in thirty seconds.

In order to explore the evolution from originality to imitation, I went first to someone who gave out a lot of work, a long-time agency music director with many years of experience in both the old jingle-oriented culture and the new pop-record mentality. I asked him to describe the prevailing creative attitude.

"Today, advertisers don't want a jingle, they want a song," he began. "Jingles, meaning an original happy melody written about a product or service that extols the benefits, qualities, and excitement that come from owning or using that product, are no longer considered *honest*. The world has changed. We have to be more honest in our advertising. More real. We use music that is real because the best ads are real. Pop songs are real. They reach the young market. Jingles do not."

I had made my living as a jingle composer, and hearing someone describe the product of my creativity as being less than honest pushed my buttons. I questioned the honesty of the "out of the room" factor of pop-song use on TV—where a viewer who is not looking directly at the screen to at least see the name and image of a product has no idea what the ad is about; and I asked about the "sound-alike" factor on radio—where the listener often can't hear a difference between the pop-song programming and the pop-song commercial. I wanted his justification for spending a client's money on a non-advertising lyric, and ending up with something that was no more memorable than supermarket music.

His answer: "Everyone is doing it; it's the accepted form; it's cutting-edge."

I pressed on. "What about trying to create your own image? Something musical that would be instantly identifiable with your client's product? Does that ever come up in the formative stages of a campaign?"

"No. And don't quote me," he said, "but in today's economic market place, it's too risky. What we're doing is original in its own way, and it's what everyone is doing. It's honest."

I didn't challenge the idea of how doing what everyone else is doing could ever be considered original, but I did want to hear his thoughts about whether the jingle would ever come back.

"Maybe," he said. "But I don't think a car or a beer will use a jingle with its name being sung anytime soon when life has changed so much. MADD, seat-belt laws, college-dorm binge-drinking, alcoholism; these are issues that the media has put front-and-center for beer manufacturers. People talk about these things at dinner, at church, at parties, all the time. And it's hard to feel that a great driving song will make you want to buy a car."

"OK," I said, "tell me what the message of 'Like a Rock . . . ' is for Chevy trucks? They've stayed with that campaign for years—a rarity in today's advertising world—and invested fortunes to establish that phrase, one of the reasons that people recognize it. Does it mean that a Chevy truck will last as long as a rock? Does it drive like a rock?" Then I joked: "Shouldn't it be 'Like a . . . cloud?' Or is it just the gravely contemporary vocal sound that everyone is in love with?"

"Bob Seegar is seen as cutting-edge by the younger potential car buyer. 'See the USA in your Chevrolet' would never work today."

We could have gone on and on—with me arguing the case for originality, and him defending the non-product-specific pop culture that pervades advertising today—but we were clearly on opposite sides of the table. And I wanted to keep his friendship.

The realization that the word "jingle" meant passé, dated, not cool, not with-it, has changed the basic lingo of the business. Composers and music producers who used to run jingle houses emphatically moved away from that word. And everyone was a little nervous.

"*Jingles* is a no-no."

"Then, what do you call yourselves?"

"We're a music house . . . I'm an advertising composer . . . a music supplier for advertising."

And: "You're not going to quote me, right?"

Fear again.

The fear of being perceived as not cutting-edge.

One theme was common to everyone: borrowed equity rules. Agencies believe that if their song comes from outside the advertising business, it's better, more genuine, and they are happy to pay huge amounts to trade on someone else's successful image rather than develop their own.

There is perhaps no better illustration of a beautifully shot, brilliantly executed commercial that fails to deliver for its client than the one that features a business man celebrating a recent triumph with his colleagues. He checks his watch, then quickly excuses himself and rushes back to his hotel room to boot up his computer in time to catch his wife giving their newborn a bath. The message is supposed to be that this particular hotel chain provides an internet connection in every room, but the non-specific pop-song lyric ("I've Got You Under My Skin") has nothing to do with the hotel. In talking with civilians about the jingle vs. pop-song issue, those who remembered the spot could not name Marriott as the sponsor. Most thought it was either for Sony, Apple, AOL, or some other computer service. One thought it was for a baby lotion. One music supplier suggested—off the record, of course—that all that was needed was a lush original-melody underscore with a lyric tagged at the end, saying something like: "The Next Best Thing to Being Home—Marriott." But, in today's terms, that would have made it a *commercial*, selling something, not a beautiful little art film. Daring to even mention that kind of approach to an agency producer might have cost the supplier a job opportunity.

The result? In their quest to be perceived as art, and not

commerce, Madison Avenue succeeds in just being bad commerce. The business manager of a major agency confided: "Sponsors have a huge problem today. The public is tuning out the ads and no one knows what to do about it." Everyone I spoke with, without exception—even on the agency side—stated, in one form or another, their opinion that the ad agency creative departments have abdicated the process of coming up with new ideas to the record industry, and specifically to the lyrics of pop songs that have nothing at all to do with the product.

The need to have advertising appear as anything *but* advertising has taken a huge toll on the income of the music supplier. What used to be an entire industry specializing in the creation of custom-made music and lyrics—jingles—is now filled with people who do little more than rearrange popular songs so they can be fitted into commercials.

The MTV quick-cut video concept was frequently identified as one of the culprits for this change in musical thinking. "The market is where the eighteen-to-thirty-fours are," an agency account supervisor said, describing the age demographic that most advertisers claim as their target audience.

One composer really nailed it: "No one thinks anymore. Imitation is the sincerest form of not having an original idea."

The crisis to come had its roots in a simpler time. In 1966, my first year in the business, TV was in its ascendancy. The three networks—CBS, NBC, and ABC—dominated the airwaves and produced every entertainment show that America watched. TV sets with thirteen channels and rabbit-ears were the state-of-the-art. Homes in most cities could only receive the network broadcasts, plus one local station. Ted Turner's cable-TV world was still a distant dream.

The impact that a single commercial could have then was enormous. If an advertiser bought network airtime, within a week the entire country would have seen the spot. This huge power created a continuing battle between the sponsors and the craft unions that represent the actors, singers, announcers, and musicians who work in commercials.

Producing jingles was a big-time business concentrated primarily in New York City, the home of Madison Avenue. When the giant corporations of America wanted big-time music tracks for their commercials, their ad agencies came to New York. Chicago and Los Angeles had smaller, but equally as competitive advertising music communities, as did Dallas, where clients went if they wanted to work non-union, meaning under-scale. But if an advertiser was willing to spend the money to sound big and important, like General Motors, he went to where GM's music suppliers worked. It was impressive for sponsors to have their music produced in New York, which not only offered the opportunity to record with the best composers, arrangers, musicians, and singers in the business, but also provided a trip to the Big Apple to see a few Broadway shows and eat at some major expense-account restaurants.

The jingle industry was then dominated by a few large production companies, and these industry leaders fought like dogs for the privilege of providing music for all the major clients: the yearly changing car accounts, the colas, the beers, the cosmetics, the detergents. Each jingle house usually had several composers and arrangers on staff, vying for the honor of representing their company in a job competition. No one ever received a salary, but everyone was nevertheless considered an exclusive part of the team, to be paid if, as, and when their jingle demo was accepted by a client to become a "final."

Jingle companies had accounts, just like agencies, that they could rely on for the stability of steady income. The musical creators of a successful ad campaign automatically expected to be rehired to produce the next flight of radio rearrangements (the rock version, the Motown version, the Latin version), as well as the background scores for all the TV spots and the annual Christmas commercial. Every ad in a campaign always used a variation of the original jingle—the melody that had become the indelible foundation of the sponsor's image— either in a full-lyric format, or just a "tag," the product's slogan sung at the end of the spot. Rarely did an ad agency take a rearranging job away from the original jingle house, only when they hired a star vocalist who preferred his/her own arranger and musicians. But even in those instances, the original supplier could participate in the income stream by supervising the recording, and making sure that the tracks all ended at the proper length. Star or no star, it was still advertising, and no one had the power to buy sixty-three seconds of airtime. (Legend has it that Helena Rubenstein, founder of the cosmetics company that bears her name, was furious with her ad agency when they informed her that they were unable to purchase sixty-three seconds of airtime for one of her commercials, even though she was more than willing to pay extra.)

The Tin Pan Alley image of songwriters toiling away in tiny rooms applied to advertising composers as well. Jingle writers were always scratching out their ideas on single-stave music paper, and then scurrying off to the ad agency conference room to present their inspirations on a guitar or on a piano that usually faced the wall. After listening to the vocal squawks and grunts that composers croaked out to demonstrate the instrumentations they envisioned in a final production, the agency critics—copywriters, art directors, producers, account types—would then pass judgment and hopefully authorize the next step: an actual recording with real musicians and singers. Sometimes, just to show ideas to the client in the early developmental stages, this took the form of a very cheap demo, using only two or three instruments and one vocalist. On rare occasions, when the ad agency was familiar with the work of the jingle house, or under an airdate deadline, they might immediately authorize a full-blown recording, but the vast majority of jobs began as demos.

Demo fees were in the $250–$500 range, and everything was spent on production costs: payments to musicians, singers, and recording studios. No jingle house could afford to have their own air-quality recording facilities—keeping up with the constantly changing cutting-edge equipment was financially impossible—so jingle producers were always making deals with their favorite independent studio, promising to give them all their work if they would charge a lower-than-rate-card fee during the demo stage. Studios never said no. They knew that part of their business was to contribute to the overall effort before the big bucks came in. The top recording rooms were always busy—everyone had their favorite audio engineer—and it was the practice of jingle producers to reserve studio time "on hold," as far in advance as possible in anticipation of landing a job.

Busy jingle houses often piggybacked several demos into one session, and used any income surpluses to pay their rent. Agency clients never cared. They never knew. No one from the agency ever showed up at demo sessions.

Composers never received a "think fee" for composing. Advertising agencies expected *thinking*—creating the lyrics and a complete melody for a jingle—to be free. When a jingle was accepted by the client as a *final*, the agency paid a "creative fee" to the winning jingle house, generally in the $2,000–$2,500 range for a national product, less for a regional advertiser. This was normally split 60–40 between the jingle house and the composer, sometimes 70–30, depending on the clout of the jingle house and the desperation of the composer.

The jingle composer always expected to be listed on the American Federation of Musicians' (AF of M) contract as the orchestra leader, along with the "studio musicians," the term for professional players who worked full-time making background tracks for advertising. If an independent musical *arranger* was required for the demo, this artist, who could take a simple melody line and make it playable by a full orchestra, received only a token fee of $50 to $100; but if he was a partner in the jingle house, no fee had to be paid. Later, the arranger of the winning jingle would also be listed on the AF of M contract, and earn $500–$750 for his part in the process.

The rewards at the end of the tunnel were easily worth any consideration during the demo stage: everyone connected with the winner knew they would qualify for union pension and welfare benefits, medical coverage, and (please rise) *residuals*, that mother of all Nirvanas, the most sought-after form of talent payment in the advertising industry.

Feeling underpaid and unappreciated is a frequent byproduct of musical success. Sometimes, composers who were winning accounts for the big jingle houses got infected with *I-want-more-of-the-pie-itis*, and would break away from their former homes to start their own companies, either in partnership with a non-musical–producer-type person, or just to work solo and handle all the business details themselves.

As the jingle industry grew, an all-important pattern was emerging: demo fees, creative fees and arranging fees, while often substantial, were becoming a secondary issue. The single enticement that was to bring about more long-term damage than any other factor was the quest for vocal residuals. And for good reason: the difference between what a union musician and a union singer could earn was astounding.

The concept of residuals for singers, actors, and announcers began in the early days of radio when everything was done *live*. Popular network programs like *The Jack Benny Show* or *Fred Allen* were actually performed twice, in front of two separate studio audiences: first for listeners in the Eastern and Central time zones; then again two hours later for the Mountain and Pacific time zones. Every line of dialogue, every song, and every joke was actually reperformed, including all the commercials. The union talent, of course, was paid twice—once for each broadcast.

One day, along came Mr. Technology, in the form of a recording machine. This gave the producer of the show the ability to retain that first performance and use it again later that night by simply pressing a button.

Management loved the new invention and immediately took the position that the actors would not have to be paid a second time since they had only worked once.

Labor hated it: actors who were formally paid for two shows were suffering a fifty-percent loss of income, while the product of their talent could potentially be used over and over without bringing the artist any additional income.

The craft unions fought back, and due in great part to the support of many big stars, achieved *residuals*; on-going payments for the reuses of their members' work. The system of residuals has been updated through the years, adapting to the invention of television, cable, and internet use; but the concept of what constitutes fair repayment for the ongoing uses of a performer's talent has been the most contentious issue in the broadcasting business ever since.

The explosive effect of residuals was felt nowhere greater than in the world of advertising. Unlike the musicians' union, which allowed thirteen weeks of unlimited use for a single residual payment—an amount roughly equivalent to a session fee—the singers' unions, Screen Actors Guild (SAG) and the American Federation of Television and Radio Artists (AFTRA), negotiated the deal of any century: when a commercial is broadcast on the networks—called Class A Use—the singers are paid for *each time the spot is aired*. (Not a misprint.) Separate and additional residuals are paid for *regional* and *local* uses, amounts determined by the size of the broadcast market and the frequency of use. Putting the mathematical gymnastics aside, the bottom line for singers is that their bottom line became humongous!

If a major advertiser produced one terrific jingle track, for example, and then used that exact track in all its commercials (which they often did), each singer in a vocal group might earn a session fee of $200 for just a few hours' work, and then receive as much as $100,000 per year for that single national campaign (again, not a misprint), with an average in the $20,000–$50,000 range. Vocal residuals for regional and local commercials could total between $5,000 and $15,000 per year, per singer, per product.

The vision of jingle singers rushing from studio to studio is not an illusion. There is no "product exclusivity" requirement for group singers, and the best vocalists often sang for Pepsi in the morning, Coke in the afternoon, and Diet Rite Cola at night; for Budweiser the next day, and Miller Beer the day after; for Ford on Monday, Pontiac on Tuesday, and . . . well, you get the picture. I worked with jingle singers who were so busy during their heyday that they had limousines standing by outside the studio—a deductible business expense, of course—just waiting to whisk them from one session to the next. One singer even had had an assistant who opened the piles of residual envelopes that arrived in the mail each day; she just didn't have the time to do it herself.

It quickly became clear that the biggest bucks for the jingle houses would be earned by composers and arrangers and partners and pals who *sang* on their commercials.

Please note: I have not mentioned the subject of vocal *talent*. Sometimes the jingle composer's greatest talent was finding a way to be listed on the union vocal report.

Finally, when the job was all done and the client was happy, and the agency was happy, and all the talent was paid and happy, the agency business department would present the jingle house with their *standard agency music contract*, within which the composer was required to sign away all rights to his creation, forever. The client owned everything, forever, including the right to reuse the jingle, forever; and to make unlimited changes in it without any additional payments to the composer or jingle house, ever again. Unlike composers in other fields of the music business (records, movies, TV themes, and background scores) who always retained some ongoing financial interest in the ongoing uses of their works, jingle composers who had received their one-time-never-to-be-repeated creative fee got nothing more. If they were unable to be listed as a singer and someone else sang their jingle, the composer got nothing. If the jingle melody was later used in an instrumental-only form, the composer got nothing. The agency was free to hire others to rearrange the jingle and to sing on it, and to completely and legally ignore the original composer as if he never existed on the face of the earth.

Having raised three children, I'm often accused of repeating myself, but I'm trying to make a vital point about what happened when a composer did not seek and retain a contractual financial interest in the future uses of his music. Ad agency business managers simply told the jingle producers that these music contracts were *standard*, and that everyone signed them. Unfortunately, they were correct.

That was the big picture: composers were singing on their tracks, and making staggering amounts in vocal residuals. The thrill of receiving a check for thousands of dollars, months and sometimes years after a job was completed had clouded any sense of long-range business smarts. Jingle producers had convinced themselves that ad agencies would continue to allow them to provide all the new rearrangements of their music, giving them that all-important ability to choose the vocalists—themselves first, of course. No one was willing to risk antagonizing the golden goose by making legal waves and asking for something positive in writing.

Why should they? They were wallowing in creative fees, arranging fees, and most of all, residuals!

No one thought the train would ever stop.

Chapter 4

How I Got Smart

I was watching *Chitty Chitty Bang Bang* with my grand-
daughter, and came away with a whole new level of appreciation for author Ian Fleming's genius.

The hero of this wonderful children's story is a man named
Caractacus Potts. Mr. Potts, played with endearing charm in
the motion picture by Dick Van Dyke, is a young widower lovingly devoted to raising his two adorable children, and is by
trade an ambitious and dedicated inventor. Though he is not
yet successful, we, the audience, know that someday he certainly will be. Family breakfasts are prepared by Rube
Goldberg–type gadgets; their clunky household, powered by a
windmill, is clogged with funny, quirky machines that make
everyone laugh, especially when they don't work, and it's all a
delicious romp headed for the inevitable happy ending.

Sure enough, one day, Potts has a terrific idea: he invents a
flute-like hard candy that actually whistles. He calls his musical toy "Toot Sweets," and tries to wrangle an appointment to

demonstrate it to a major candy manufacturer.

At first, he is left to cool his heels in the waiting room, unable to even get passed the dismissive secretary. But the owner of the company, a bulbous, gruff titan of industry, has a beautiful daughter named Truly Scrumptious, and she takes pity on Potts and asks Papa to give him an audition.

Unfortunately, his invention is rejected, but Potts and Truly fall in love—they don't know it yet, but we do.

To make a long story short—as is necessary in advertising—near the end of the film, just when things are looking their bleakest, the candy mogul rushes in and announces to Potts that he wants to manufacture the musical whistle—hooray!—not only because of its unique flavor, but also because it attracts dogs so easily. Further, exercising his rights as the client, he has renamed the product "Woof Sweets," probably as the result of some in-depth focus-group testing.

Potts is ecstatic, thrilled, and delighted.

Daddy Candy then pulls out a multi-page contract.

At this point, the movie takes a brief left-turn while Potts rushes off to tell Truly that he loves her, so he doesn't actually sign the agreement onscreen. But we all know it's a done deal, and that he and Truly and the children will then spend the rest of their days laughing and singing and flying around in their magical car, Chitty Chitty Bang Bang. (At least that's what we think when the movie ends: Mr. Fleming, creator of James Bond, Agent 007, doesn't tell us what it's going to be like when Potts has to go to work every day for his wife's father in the family candy business; but we don't have to project that far.)

And they all live happily ever after.

And it's just a super-special, heart-warming story.

And everyone goes home smiling.

The end.

Next haircut.

WAITAMINUTE!

Did Potts read the contract before he signed it?
Did he understand its terms?
Did he ask a lawyer to represent him?

Was it an employee-for-hire deal where Potts owns nothing, and the Candy Man owns everything? Or is Potts just licensing the toy for a limited amount of time, after which he retains the rights to license it again to a different candy company?

Will he receive only a one-time fee for his creation, or will he get a royalty for every whistle that is sold?

Did he indemnify the candy company against every possible alleged breach in sugar-tooth land—including all the cavities that kids around the world might get, even though the candy company carries its own malpractice insurance policy and Potts can't afford one?

Will the candy be produced under union conditions? And if so, can Potts put his name on the union contract and qualify for pension and medical coverage?

Questions, questions, questions . . .

Now, Ian Fleming was no dope. He named his lead character Cracked Pot (it says here) not only because he was an eccentric inventor, but also as a sly and astute commentary about how artistic types with no legal experience are typically treated in the world of big business. Mr. Fleming knew that a naïve, innocent, trusting soul like Potts would never dare ask questions about the deal, and buck the system, and risk the wrath of his potential benefactor. No way. Guaranteed: Potts inked that standard form parchment the moment he got back.

I didn't have any business background either, but I never wanted to be considered a cracked pot, not if I could help it. I wanted to learn about all that stuff and those were the kind of questions I always asked, even though the answers sometimes got me into big trouble.

I entered the advertising music business through the back door at the age of twenty-nine, after spending ten years as an entertainer (I'm an Arthur Godfrey Talent Scout Show loser, and never had a hit record), including the last three trying to change directions by composing the background scores for low-budget porno movies. These films usually had wall-to-wall music—"needle drops," library recordings that were mostly stolen, rarely paid for. The producer who gave me my first film job, an industrious gentleman named Barry Mahon, believed that the addition of something custom-made would enhance the quality of his work. I was lucky: his pride in having an "original music score," rare in this type of cheapy movie, became my chance to learn.

The recordings were all done monaural (mono). Stereophonic had become the standard in the record industry for 33⅓-rpm vinyl albums; FM radio stations, the new kid in town, could broadcast in stereo; but movie theaters only had mono sound systems capable of playing a single track mix of dialogue, effects, and music.

Music for advertising was mono, too. The network television broadcasts actually ran 35mm film prints of commercials, while 16mm *reductions* were sent out to stations across the country that didn't have the high-end equipment to play 35mm.

My movie-score orchestras were usually five or six terrific young players, newcomers like myself who wanted to break into the New York recording scene any way they could. Everyone agreed to work non-union—green money paid right on the session—and since I could not offer them the protection of being a union signatory, I always made sure to get a check from my movie producer at least forty-eight hours before the date. As soon as it was in hand, I headed straight for the bank to cash it. The first time I asked for the check before 3 PM, Barry raised an eyebrow; but I made it clear that while I trusted his word, the players I was hiring on his behalf wouldn't. He understood, and we never had a problem. I just learned never to book anything *firm-firm* until two days before the date. A few times I was suckered into deferring my own portion of the deal for thirty days—it usually took much longer than that to get paid—but I figured that if that I was straight with the band, they would work with me again. I also paid the studio bill in cash, and always before the session. I might not have been a large-dollar client, but I wanted everyone to know that I was reliable in honoring my obligations. If I netted $200 per film, it was a lot. However, in perspective, the rent on my small Brooklyn apartment was $83 a month, so I squeaked by, occasionally with a little help from my parents. I also made it my own parental obligation to buy a US Savings Bond for each of my infant children from the *profit* of each film, writing their individual names and the title of the movie on the corner of the document. A $25 savings bond then cost $18.75, and matured in seven years. I gave these tokens from my scoring career to my delighted and surprised kids years later when they were in college. They were as happy with the memories as I was.

It was in this steamy world of underground show business that I learned the real beginnings of craft. I would spend hours at the Moviola (a film editing device now replaced by an Avid), trying to develop musical styles that would be appropriate for the onscreen action, which was mostly outdoor travelogue shots of photographers on their way to take brief pictures of naked ladies. Linda Lovelace had not yet appeared on the scene, and inventing music to accompany these innocuous activities became quite a challenge.

Barry was a realist, caring little about the artistic quality of his films, ultimately concerned only that they came in at the minimally acceptable length—sixty-five minutes—and that he could produce them cheaply enough and show enough flesh to attract a distributor. Besides, in the semi-lit theaters where they played, the sound systems were usually so old that everything distorted anyway. To put it in advertising terms: from the consumer point of view, the prime focus was on the visual portion of the product, and not the audio.

My deal was to work within whatever modest budget Barry had, and also to own the copyrights for all the music. They were of no real value to him anyway, and though they would not produce any additional income for me, I thought it would be a way to build a reputation as a music publisher.

Our studio sessions were a mad scramble to record everything in one take—there was no budget for retakes—and this placed great demands on the stamina of my musicians and sound engineer. We never recorded Hollywood-style, actually viewing the picture while we played, something that brought endless groans from my band when I could only describe the onscreen action. Barry had taught me the tricks of using a stopwatch to determine when a track had to end, and if I made errors a simple cross-fade in the film mix became a savior to this novice Mancini. Sometimes, if a particular track was too long, Barry would show me where the tape could be cut, literally with a razor blade. After a few films, he let me do the cutting myself—he was usually too busy trying to raise money to produce more films. If my track ended up on the short side, I had the freedom to actually edit the picture. Such is the exacting art of composing for skin-flicks.

In one film, a group of traveling salesmen were seen sitting on a funky couch in someone's living room ogling a few ladies perform a striptease. This particular scene ran for ten minutes—*ten full minutes* of the same three women dancing around and around while the men just sat there—not touching, just watching. The monotony was occasionally broken up by a different camera angle, but there was no music playback system on the set, and from time to time I could hear Barry's voice (he was also the cameraman) yelling at the girls to keep moving! If you think the men on the couch got tired of watching, and the girls got tired of dancing, you can imagine how the band felt.

For this epic, Barry wanted to depart from the clichéd, bluesy, stripper music typical in this kind of scene, and he ordered something different: belly-dance music, complete with oboe, finger bells, tabla drums, and sitar-like sounds. The Beatles were entering their Ravi Shankar stage and Barry wanted to be cutting-edge. I had prepared a lead sheet which could be played over and over until the required ten minutes had been filled up. This worked out well for me: I just kept focus on my stop watch. It was a different experience, however, for my oboe player. After a few choruses his eyes began pleading with me to tell him that the time had expired. Ten minutes of *boom-ditty-boom-ditty-boom-ditty* seemed like eternity. It was like falling asleep on a long plane flight, and waking up seven hours later to find out that there are still five more hours to go. It was endless!

In another movie (I had branched out and was working for several different exploitation film magnates), I was able to convince one of my producers to give me enough money for a larger-than-usual band—I was always pushing the envelope. I had not yet mastered the art of arranging, especially orchestrating for strings, so I asked my high school band trumpet player, Dick Behrke, who was a better technical musician than me, to do the charts for the sections I couldn't handle. Dick went on to have his own career in advertising as one of the finest arranger-composers in the business. The film was called *Party Girls for the Candidate*, and starred Mamie Van Doren, who was married to top bandleader Ray Anthony, and Ted Knight, who later went on to fame as Mary Tyler Moore's newsroom sidekick, Ted Baxter. (Everyone starts somewhere, right?)

Our sound engineer at Associated Recording in New York, Larry Schnapf, had an Ampex four-track machine in his studio that was used for all record dates done there. But this latest technological marvel—offering the ability to record four separate tracks at the same time, or just record one and overdub three—required the additional expense of special half-inch tape, and necessitated equal time to remix everything back down to the mono format that was required for the movie theatres. When I suggested to my producer that he allow extra money for this extra artistic flexibility, his immortal words made clear his level of priority: "Steve, nobody listens to the music in a porno movie." Humbled, but resolute, we worked in mono. What you heard was what you got. (I once had six features running at the same time on 42nd Street, then the Mecca for sleaze in New York. I doubt that Bill Conte or John Williams ever had as good a track record. Nor would they write about it if they did!)

A cameraman who was moonlighting in my soft-porn world was also daylighting in advertising, and gave my name to an agency producer who was looking for *something different*. (This is starting to sound familiar, isn't it?)

When I stepped on to Madison Avenue, I was known as "the new," someone who could write a good melody and was willing to work cheap.

My first commercial was a public service spot for the Girl Scouts—it would be broadcast in the middle of the night for a few months—and I recorded it at Associated Studios, where I was by then affectionately called the "king of the porn flicks." There, at least I was comfortable with the surroundings and engineer, removing another source of pre-session anxiety. I wrote for a folk guitar (played by Walter Raim, another member of my old high school band who went on to a successful career as a respected arranger/composer in advertising), and a harmonica, played by Mike Chimes, a highly regarded musical giant, willing to take the non-union job because there were not a lot of session calls for harmonica players. The track was a pre-recorded 60-second TV spot—the film editor would cut his commercial to the music afterwards.

The film's producer, David Funt, was pleased with my work, and gave me a list of contacts in the ad agency world, suggesting that I put together a music reel to demonstrate my ability to compose for advertising. Ad agencies were always looking for something new for their clients and definitely had more money to spend on music than producers of porn films, a lesson I learned on more than one occasion when a musician would cancel on me at the last minute because he had been called to record a jingle, which was a union job that paid more and had the potential of residuals. Approaching the new world of advertising, I figured that if I could write sixty-five minutes of music for a movie, a 60-second commercial would be a piece of cake.

I began my presentation reel with my latest hit, the two-man-band Girl Scout spot, followed by six or seven of the best short hunks from my nudie movies—the chase scene from the horror porn, *The Beautiful, the Bloody and the Bare*; the dance sequence from *I Was a Girl on a Chain Gang*; the sad melancholy cello ending from *The Twisted Sex*. I began hanging around at friendly film studios to meet agency producers while they shot commercials. I made cold phone calls to names that I found by reading the industry trade papers, *Backstage* and *Ad Age*:

"Hi, my name is Steve Karmen, and I'm a new composer with lots of experience in scoring motion pictures. (Sounds impressive, doesn't it?) Can I make an appointment so you can listen to my advertising reel?"

"I don't have time to listen to reels with composers in the room. Mail it in."

"Is there anyone else who might listen? I really don't have

a lot of copies. Couldn't you find eight minutes to discover a new musical genius who can help make your job easier?" (My reel was longer than eight minutes, but when you're listening to great stuff, the time just *flies* by.)

Click.

Sometimes, when I was able to talk my way in, I would ask for other names to pursue for work at that agency. Thanks to my pals at Associated, I had additional presentation reels made and could now leave a copy when requested.

I hope you're getting the picture of the networking that was and is necessary for any beginner.

By now, and again with the help of my parents, I had purchased a small house in Rockville Center, Long Island, New York. With a wife and three young daughters, the pressure to earn a living was enormous. I did everything I could to remain in the music business: I wrote parody songs for other singers; I did $50 singing club dates on weekends; I painted friends apartments to make extra cash; anything to avoid giving up.

A young neighbor across the street, Werner Koopmann, had just opened his own small film company, Totem Productions, and was working on a commercial for one of the big time ad agencies, Benton and Bowles Advertising. He got me an appointment with their music director, Roy Eaton, who sat stoically and listened to my reel.

Roy was a classically trained musician with a no-nonsense reputation. This was clearly not a job where I would be able to fake my way musically and then re-edit the film myself later. But he was willing to take a chance, and when we met at the film editor's to "take counts," I learned how little I actually knew about film scoring. ("Taking counts" is the process of measuring the film by individual frames to determine where specific actions occur: the door slams at 14 feet 8 frames; the lips touch at 43 feet 12 frames, and so on.)

The spot was a 30-second commercial for Maxwell House

Coffee, which was being packaged in a specially shaped, clear-glass jar. The object was to illustrate the many uses that could be made of this wondrous jar: first it was a place to putt a golf ball, then a fish tank complete with splashing goldfish, then a flowerpot, then a piggybank. The list went on and on—sixteen different uses, sixteen different *hits*, all in thirty seconds.

Roy sat with me and we discussed his concept of what should happen and which instrumentation I should use. Naturally, wanting to be agreeable, *his* concept immediately became *my* concept. He suggested I use a harpsichord, going for a classical approach with a little rock flavoring thrown in. Then he gave me the names of some studio musicians (Bernie Leighton to play the harpsichord, Milt Hinton to play the bass, Chico Hamilton to play the drums), and suggested that I book them for the session. Before this, I had only worked with players who were my friends.

As I watched the film counter zip by, filling my page with the numbers of all the quick hits, noting Roy's thoughts about what should happen at each point, I realized that I was terribly unprepared to handle this enormous job. Oh, I could write the music without any problem, I thought, but I certainly did not have the technique to guarantee that my arrangement would catch the hits each time.

After Roy left, I stayed to talk the film editor.

"Want standard punching?" he asked.

I decided not to fake it. "What's that?"

He had sensed my inexperience. "Four singles and a double—that's where the music starts. A single warning at the end, and then a double at the end of sound."

"How do you determine what the right tempo is to make the hits?"

"Compose at any tempo that has a whole number of frames—no fractions—and watch the holes go by during the leader. I can punch them ten frames apart, eleven, nine, eight, whatever you want. The holes will be your tempo guide. If the studio has the equipment, get them to set up an extra monitor near the drummer. It helps when two people see the starting punches."

I agreed to call him as soon as I established a tempo for my music.

My most serious problem had yet to be confronted: I knew of no way to determine from the counts where the hits would actually occur in the music.

I called a musician who had composed scores for some industrial films. "How do you determine how many beats of music it takes to get to a certain place in the film?"

"I watch the picture and use my pocket metronome set to the tempo I want, then I clock it on my stopwatch until I reach the hit. Try to use full-frame tempos like nine, ten, eleven— it's easier to punch the film." (This confirmed the editor's remarks.) He then described how to convert the frames into metronome settings.

"But how do you know that these spring-wound clocks are accurate, especially on occasions when the cues are really close together?"

"Oh, I adjust it after, by eye, on the session. It's usually only a beat or two here and there."

I could not imagine taking the time on a session to adjust a music track with sixteen cues to catch. It would take forever and cost a fortune while the musicians sat around and watched me do homework.

My friendly film editor suggested that I call the president of a major jingle house, with whom he had done a lot of work. I naïvely expected the same sense of camaraderie that I enjoyed with my own musicians, who always guided me through technical matters when I got in over my head. I introduced myself, and asked if he would share what he knew about finding out where the hits are.

He replied brusquely that I represented competition to his company and it would not be appropriate to share anything with me, especially technical information. When I explained that I was just starting out, doing my first job, and was not in his exalted league, and merely wanted to ask some questions and not steal business, it was to no avail. Without an apology, he hung up.

In desperation, I needed someone to talk to who might help me puzzle through the problem. I called my father, who was a civil engineer working for the City of New York, and really good at math.

I explained the situation.

"How fast does the film move?" he asked.

"Twenty-four frames per second. The counts are measured in feet and frames."

"How many frames to a foot?"

"Sixteen frames per foot."

"What tempo do you want to use?"

"One hundred twenty beats per minute would be okay, that's twelve frames per beat. But what if I want to change the tempo?"

"One problem at a time," he said patiently, promising to call back as soon as he had a solution. Twenty minutes later the phone rang.

"At a tempo of 120 beats per minute the golf ball hits the jar in nine-and-a-half beats . . . it's eleven beats to where the fish jumps, thirteen-and-a-quarter to the flower pot . . . "

"How did you do that?" I asked, suddenly relieved and mightily impressed.

"Give me a few days," my father said, "and I'll develop a chart you can use."

On the day of the session, I arrived at the studio an hour early and asked the projectionist to run the film over and over so I could get accustomed to watching the punches go by.

Needless to say I hit every cue, thanks to my father's ability to invent a workable formula; and the track I wrote was accepted by the Maxwell House client.

In order to prepare for more jobs, I expanded my father's charts for every setting on my metronome. It took two years to complete. I later learned that there were books in existence that had already done all the calculating, and in much greater detail, breaking down tempos into eighths-of-a-frame to conform to the new digital metronome that had become the industry standard. But throughout my entire career I always used my own books and my father's system.

The Maxwell House commercial didn't run long, just enough for the jar promotion. There was no way to measure the effectiveness of my music on product sales, but its positive impact on my professional life was indelible.

The only negative was that Roy Eaton never again considered me for work at Benton and Bowles, even after I was well established in the industry. There must have been some personality rub between us that didn't sit well with him; perhaps that the young green kid he had squired through his first job had gone on to big success with his own company, and that he, the schooled master, was still working for someone else. Years later, I ran into Roy and asked why he never called. "Oh, there was nothing I thought you were right for," he said. I left it at that.

Now that I had a real commercial under my belt, I added it to the top of my presentation reel, and started to get other jobs, composing background scores for Lucky Whip Topping, Pepperidge Farm Bread, Super Stripe Toothpaste, and Dove Liquid. When agencies found out that I could also write lyrics, I did campaigns for Fina Gasoline, Scotch Guard, and Johnson's Baby Oil. By this time, my company, Elsmere Music, had become a signatory to the union codes.

One day, after I had completed a spot for Score Haircream,

I was summoned to the office of Grey Advertising's creative director Manning Rubin, who inquired if I would be interested in the job of Grey's music director. This was a great compliment for a beginning composer. My responsibilities would be to oversee all of Grey's music production. I wouldn't be able to compose as much but this kind of job would certainly solidify my income situation with a weekly salary plus all the other benefits that go with full-time employment. I had no experience in the corporate world, and when I hesitated, Manning asked me to think it over, and to meet with Marc Brown, the owner of one of the largest jingle houses in the business, who might give me some advice.

Marc drove a Rolls Royce convertible, and owned a weekend house in the Hamptons, so he certainly knew how the business worked. Kermit Levinsky, Walt Levinsky, and Tommy Newsome were heavyweight writers and arrangers who worked exclusively for his company. The legend about Marc Brown is that he once sent a bill to a client for a key change. It seemed that on the session, which was recorded live in those mono days before overdubbing, the singer couldn't make the high note, and the band had to play the music a tone lower. With great studio musicians, simply asking, "Can we please try this a tone lower?" always works. They just play it, no sweat. But for an unknowing, unsuspecting ad agency producer, and an even more remotely removed client, this difficult, over-budget key change became a billable item.

Marc questioned me about my background, laughed about my porno-score experiences, and listened to the first three spots on my reel. "Don't take the job; you'll do better on your own."

Instead of being put out when I turned him down, Manning gave me a package of work that really put my company solidly in business: he offered $36,000 if I would provide the background tracks for thirty-six separate Celanese Fabric commercials that Grey had to produce during the next year— $1,000 per spot, to include union musicians, pensions, etc., and all studio costs. He expected first class productions, meaning no two-man bands, but whatever was left would be profit. Of course, I took the job. The musicians' union permitted the recording of three spots for each hour of scale payment, and Manning agreed to wait until three commercials had been filmed and edited before I was required to do a session.

A week after we shook hands on the deal, a check arrived, payable to my company, in the amount of $18,000. Half in advance, unprecedented in the jingle industry. My hand trembled as I counted all the zeros. When I called Manning to say thanks, he said it was a vote of confidence that I would do a terrific job for Celanese. I've been in business ever since, and I can still feel the glow.

As I my career gained speed, I began developing my own working habits to conform to the needs of my clients while trying not to ignore my wife and family. I've always been fascinated by how other writers work, and I'm forever asking questions; not about which comes first—the music or the lyrics— but about the nuts and bolts of being a songwriter, about professional techniques, and how being a composer translates into a day-to-day lifestyle.

I know this will sound odd, but I prefer to write music with a red Scripto pencil containing a soft black IBM computer lead, which makes darker lines the harder it is pressed—especially great for score pads. This lead is also easy to erase— especially great when I make mistakes. An old-time song writer gave me a red pencil in the beginning of my career, and I guess I thought it brought me luck. One day, when it started to break, I ordered six gross—in boxes of twelve—884 red pencils. My secretary thought I was nuts, but I never wanted to run out of red pencils. I've just checked my closet, and after thirty years, there are forty-eight unused pencils left—four boxes—in addition to the many that are spread out in my work studio and throughout my house and writing world. I hope there will be enough to last through the ride home. I still have that first pencil, now literally broken in half and unusable—it sits in my pencil box where I see it every time I go to work.

I'm an early person. I like to create early, often beginning my working day at 5 AM. By 10 AM, when the world starts to wake up and intrude on my solitude, I've already got half a day's writing done. When I learned that the musicians' union permitted a session to begin at 8 AM without any overtime charges, I began booking players at that hour. Musicians, by trade, are not early risers, and for some cats 8 AM is considered the middle of the night. Top studio musicians are usually booked through a central answering service, and are always playing on an 10-to-11 with a "possible twenty" overtime; a 12-to-2; a 3-to-5; and a 7-to-10 for the producers who like to record at night. When my first 8 AM call went out, every player double-checked with their service to confirm it was not an 8 PM booking. (In New York, an 8 AM session was groundbreaking; in Los Angeles, where they score movies, 8 AM is the standard start time.) Then, there were the issues of dealing with rush-hour traffic; finding a place to park; and getting to the studio in time to set up and warm up to be ready for a downbeat   at 8 AM. There were no complaints: when the players realized that they could do my session and then be out in time to make someone else's 10 or 10:30 AM start—thereby increasing their chances for more residuals—everyone's eyes were twinkling again, even though they were a bit bloodshot.

My career-long practice was to arrive at the studio an hour before a session was scheduled to begin, just in case there were any last minute changes in the music or re-edits in the film I was scoring, and to confirm that any special instruments I might have rented were delivered on time. Often, the assistant engineer, the person who sets up the microphones, would sleep in the control room the night before just to be ready for my early start.

I also wanted to be on the job before my client arrived. Sometimes the agency producers complained about my early habits, but I resisted starting at a more human hour. Molding a big orchestra into delivering a precise 60- and 30-second performance is not an exact science; it takes a cauldron of coffee, a platter of bagels and donuts, the joke-of-the-day, and a professional attitude to keep the level of musical enthusiasm high. Starting early provided me with an hour or so alone to perfect my rhythm section tracks without someone breathing down my neck.

I kept a standing offer: I would buy breakfast for anyone who would show up at 7 AM; and the coffee shop next door to my favorite studio was usually busy with my basic band, all gobbling down bacon, eggs, and coffee, waking up, getting ready to work. Wally Dunbar copied, clarified, and made beautiful every score I have ever orchestrated. Billy Slapin, my contractor, hired the same musicians all the time, my musical family. Ronnie Zito was my drummer for my whole career; Moe Wechslor played piano; any combination of Jay Berliner, Eric Weissberg, Stu Scharf, Sal DiTroia, Jon Tropea, or Vinnie Bell played guitar; Ralph MacDonald, Dave Carey, and Jack Jennings were always on percussion; when synthesizers became part of the music scene, Pete Cannarozzi joined the band. These wonderful artists always made my music sound better: they knew how I liked to work, and I had complete confidence in their talent and flexibility, an invaluable asset on the occasions when I had to make a fast adjustment to accommodate a change requested by my client.

The coffee-shop gang, however, rarely included my bass player. I've worked with some of the great masters of that instrument, and all over the world, but I've found that, as a breed, bass players are notoriously late, something that is unacceptable in advertising. Maybe it has to do with the head that it takes to be at the bottom of the band, but bassists invariable do not make an entrance until downbeat time. Or a few moments after. In the days before overdubbing, where everyone in the orchestra played *live* at the same time, that first run-through for a client's ears was critical in making the right impression. Without the bass, the music sounded empty. One particular bass player I worked with was always fifteen minutes late, and I mean *always*. He was a very good musician, and I liked the way he played my music so I tolerated his excuses for a long time, much longer than the rest of the band thought was necessary. He was having problems at home, and I wanted to show understanding. A big part of being a professional musician, however, particularly in advertising music, is honoring the commitment to show up and be ready to work on time. In the pop-record business, where each union-scale payment permits three hours of work, players often drift into the studio somewhere near the appointed hour when the spirit moves them, and then they hang out for awhile, chatting, having coffee, getting in the mood, and it's all acceptable loosy-goosy; but this was advertising, where clients don't care if a musician is fighting with his wife. The mood starts with the downbeat, at the time of the booking, not later. To my other musicians, this habitual latecomer had become a standing joke; but in front of a client paying the bills it was never funny. Finally, contractor Billy Slapin decided to teach him a lesson: we hired the entire orchestra for a 10 AM start (in the days before my 8 AM adventures) and the bass player alone for 9:30. Billy instructed any early arrivals to wait in the next studio. At 9:15, I started to worry; why was I going through this exercise just to make a point to someone who should have known better. Maybe I should just begin using a different player. By 9:30, he still hadn't appeared. 9:35; 9:40. At 9:45, the door opened and my bass player rushed in, his head low, as usual, to avoid the glares of the others. He went right to his chair, sat down, unzipped the case of his electric bass, plugged into his amplifier, turned it on, and then looked up. There was no one in the room. We let him sit like that for a few minutes. Puzzled, he pulled out his date book to check about the time. At 9:50 we all came in and ignored him, getting ready to start the session. He apologized later, but after he did the same thing once more, Billy insisted that I find a more reliable player. He was right—it was not fair to the others.

A composer with power to give out work falls into one of three categories: he's either loved by those musicians he hires, to whom every note he writes is a gem; or he's jealously dismissed from a distance by those he has yet to hire; or he is hated with a vengeance by those with whom he has once worked, but does not call again. Not being re-called is perceived as an insult in front of the entire musical community. A French horn player that I used a few times early in my career fit solidly into that last category.

He was an old pro, and I had initially hired him on the recommendation of a colleague. When he played as part of an ensemble he sounded just fine. Then, once, I was asked to write for an airline, and the agency wanted to begin their three-minute presentation version with a twenty-five-second French horn solo as the plane rose through the clouds and burst into the sunlight. I booked this player along with a forty-piece orchestra. I had written a challenging part, long sustained tones building to a harp-sweep into the full orchestra. There were two additional horn players on the session, but I assigned him the solo. When we began to rehearse, my clients came into the studio from the control room to listen. After a few run-throughs of playing naked in front of the entire orchestra, the player's lips began to quiver, the worst thing for a French horn. Instead of a long smooth BAAAAAAAAA, it became a stuttered BA-A-A-A-A-A-A-A-A. Out of concern for wearing him down, I instructed him to *lay-out* while I rehearsed the other sections of this long piece. This only added to his pressure. In a later era, when there would be the ability to overdub instruments, this would never have been a problem. I could have just asked him not to play the opening; we would have recorded everything else, and I would have added him separately at the end of the session, in an empty studio, and it would have been accomplished perfectly in one or two takes.

Things only got worse when we were ready to record. During his opening solo, he began to crack, and we had to start again. And again. Each time I said, "One more time, please," as softly and politely as possible, he sounded weaker and weaker, retreating into himself. Since he was the only one playing while thirty-nine other musicians sat around, listening, I struggled with the idea of passing the part to a different horn player, which would have been humiliating for him. He was a heavyset man, and was now sweating profusely.

When we finally got a complete performance, the orchestra applauded, making light of his ordeal, which only compounded his embarrassment. Later, in the control room, my client snidely joked that *next time I ought to hire someone who could play the part.* Clients don't concern themselves with the human side of music—all they know is what they pay for.

In the next few days, other players called Billy, recommending names of the new young strong French horn players in town.

We didn't book the old-timer again. I felt badly about it, but I had no choice. I had lost confidence in his ability. From then on, every time I saw him on the street, he would cross to the other side to avoid acknowledging me.

Afull day's recording session could begin at 8 AM and end after midnight. The rhythm section played first, from 8 to 10; the synthesizer and timpani overdubs until 10:30; the brass and reeds from 10:30 to noon; the strings from noon to 2 PM; the vocals from 2 to 4; and the audio mix—where we put all the layers together into one cake—from 4 PM until whenever. Billy once said that there was real-time and Karmen-time. I was invariably behind schedule. (Finding a moment to go to the bathroom was not easy; I've often said that one of the keys to success in the jingle business was the ability to *hold it*.)

There were always crowds of people waiting their turn in the hallway. The singers, typically the last group to be over-dubbed, often sat around for hours, chattering away about their stock portfolios and who was sleeping with whom, never complaining unless they had accepted someone else's later session and had a conflict. But their concerns were always coated with sugar: the rewards of residuals were too enormous to ever risk offending anyone.

Whenever I was working on a secret project, particularly when helping an advertising agency in a competition to win an account, I would book the vocalists without revealing the name of the product, simply calling the job "Project X." (Musicians never cared whether it was Beethoven or Bisquick, as long as they got paid on time.) When word was out that an account was up for grabs, several jingle houses in the competition often hired the same top singers. I didn't think it necessary to reveal what I was working on, but the singers felt differently. A "Project X" booking would usually generate a call from the singers' answering service, inquiring if it was a demo or a final. This was the singers' way of wanting to choose between a small job that might never be broadcast and a national spot that could pay for a Cadillac, or three. I always instructed Billy to respond, "Life is a demo." No one ever turned down a date.

In the studio I knew what I wanted to achieve: it was always about the music. Sometimes, I know, it came off as *attitude*.

There were occasions when I was forced to stop in the middle of the quiet string rehearsal because my agency client decided to make a loud phone call, or discuss the ball scores while we were practicing difficult vocal articulation. "I don't come to your office and make phone calls while you work," I would say, as diplomatically as possible, "and the same courtesy would be appropriate here." The resulting calm would usually last for about three minutes, then the yakking would resume. At that point, I would instruct the sound engineer to raise the overall speaker volume in the control room.

"It's very loud in here," the offender would say. "I can't hear what I'm saying."

"We can." Then, I'd tell everyone to *take five*.

"Why aren't we working?"

"Just waiting for your attention."

Sometime they got it, sometimes not.

Once, I had to actually ask a client's representative to leave a session because he was way out of line with his commentary. I had never met him before. He had not attended any of the pre-production meetings. He just showed up after we had started recording—Mr. Big Shot—and began ordering changes that were completely contrary to the directions I had been given by the agency before the job began. *Make the tempo slower, I want to hear more drums, that guitar figure is too busy, the piano is too loud.* There was no stifling the endless expression of his expertise. The orchestra was sitting in the studio, on the other side of the glass, wondering what all the gesturing in the control room was about. I simply refused to continue unless he left. When he finally huffed out, the agency producers apologized. A recording session is a fun experience, and for the sake of the music, it was the right thing to do. A positive working atmosphere can add much to the quality of the final spot. Certainly, there are always changes to be made, and I know that the client ultimately pays the bill; but I also believe it's inappropriate for the patient to give instructions to the surgeon in the middle of an operation.

From a distance it sounds harsh, but I knew what I had to do, and what I was being paid for, and there is little time to waste when the orchestra's overtime is measured in twenty-minute increments.

Talk about attitude on the job: I often think of the "I Love New York" commercial that featured Frank Sinatra. His particular segment, part of the enormously successful series of New York State tourism spots about Broadway shows, was to be filmed outdoors in Times Square, beneath the statue of George M. Cohan. Frank wasn't going to sing, just speak one simple line of dialogue directly into the camera, while the cast of the hit show *Cats* wriggled all around him. I had prepared a special eight-second prerecorded track, and we began rehearsing at 7 PM on a summer's evening. Frank was scheduled to do his part at midnight. *Five hours* to rehearse an eight-second hunk of film! Over and over everyone practiced: they set the lights, they changed the lights; they debated the camera angle, they readjusted the angle; the put big Cats next to Frank's stand-in, then they tried little Cats; the client looked into the camera, the agency producers looked into the camera; they had meetings; they broke for dinner; then they readjusted the lights, readjusted the angle, readjusted the Cats, on and on and on. In the meantime, the agency suit-types were keeping Frank lubricated at the 21 Club, one of New York's finest upscale restaurants, just in case he might pull a "Sinatra," and decided to go home. Finally, at ten past twelve, after we had rehearsed at least fifty times, an unmarked car pulled up, and accompanied by the Chief of Police, out stepped Ol' Blue Eyes, dressed in a tuxedo, making it clear with his attitude that he was doing everyone a huge favor by deigning to appear in a lowly commercial. Director Stan Dragotti gave Frank his line, positioned him among the Cats, and yelled, "Action!"

His demeanor changed instantly. Out came the Sinatra smile, the Sinatra charm, the Sinatra sparkle.

It was done. Frank started to walk off.

"We need one more, please."

"Why? Did I blow my line?"

"No, but we'd like to have one more."

Frank continued to walk.

"*Please*, Frank, give us one more. For insurance."

There was an instant of panic when everyone thought that Frank would actually leave. But he turned, and went back to the statue.

"Action!"

This time, meaner than a junkyard dog, he didn't come back. Gone. He had done his part. He didn't schmooze the client, shake hands with the Cats, nothing. He knew what they wanted, what had to be done, and he had delivered.

When I tell people about that night, they often ask if I met Frank Sinatra. "I certainly did," I always ad lib. "He talked to me."

"Really? Wow! What did he say?"

"Well, I stuck out my hand, and said 'Hi, Frank, I'm Steve Karmen, the composer of 'I Love New Yor...'"

"And he said, 'Get the hell out of my way!'"

Now *that's* workplace attitude!

Halo Shampoo changed my life." It sounds like a copy line, but in my case it was true.

A 30-second TV spot that would run on the network for less than thirteen weeks was to have the biggest impact on the way I did business of anything that has ever happened in my professional career.

Halo Shampoo used a jingle, written before World War II,

which had been their standard-bearer forever. "Halo, Everybody, Halo," was easily as well known to consumers as "Mmm Mmm Good" was for Campbell Soups. The TV spot I was asked to work on would be a rearrangement of this classic jingle.

The visual began with a shot of an old phonograph playing a scratchy 78-rpm ancient-sounding recording of "Halo, Everybody, Halo." A hand enters the picture, grabs the record, rips it off the turntable, smashes it to pieces, and the announcer says, "Stop! There's a *new* Halo . . . "

A group of girls, à la the Supremes, continues the jingle, in a hip modern way, accompanied by a hip cutting-edge background track, all extolling the virtues of the *new* Halo Shampoo, which was now shown on the screen. It would be thirty seconds of fun.

Finding the right girls was easy. I booked three of the new-era jingle singers, Valerie Simpson, Jean Thomas-Fox, and Leslie Miller; and, since it really didn't matter who sang the *old* Halo voice because it was going to be squashed and equalized down to nothing anyway, befitting a worn-out 78-rpm record, I sang it myself.

Everyone loved it.

It went on the air, and the client was very happy.

I had been paid a total of $250 to write the arrangement, and my name appeared on the musicians' contract as leader (earning $72) and as arranger ($50, scale). My total income for attending the preproduction meeting at the agency, for visiting the editing house to see the film, for writing the chart, for conducting and supervising the session, for making sure the mix was perfect, for returning to the editing house to confirm that the music was synced up to the film properly, for taking the agency producer to lunch afterwards, and for doing all the things that a concerned business person would do to please his client, was $372.

A few weeks later (within the first fifteen working days, as required by the Screen Actors Guild union agreement), I received a check in the mail from William Esty Advertising, Halo's agency, paying me for my singing part: $1,600!

$1,600 for basically just walking into the studio, smiling at everyone, singing three lines of lyric, smiling some more, and then leaving.

That's what the singers did.

Boys and girls, there was something wrong with this picture.

This was to be my first exposure to the juicy rewards of the vocal residual.

I began to ask around, but jingle producers didn't want to talk about this particular subject. Then, I learned from the *real* jingle singers that it was the ongoing practice for the music house composer/arranger/employee/sister/secretary/book-keeper to add their names to the SAG and AFTRA vocal contracts so they could qualify for union residuals. It certainly made sense. But did all of these people actually stand in front of a microphone and emote?

One time, I happened to be in the same building where a colleague was doing a vocal overdub in the next studio and I stopped in to wave hello. I noticed that the microphone setup was quite unusual: yes, there were the traditional boys and girls facing each other across their music stands, each group on their own mike. My colleague, however, the jingle house composer, was standing between them, his back to the control room window so no one in the booth could see his face, and he was singing into his own special microphone. Does anyone want to guess whether his mike was turned on? Was he really in the studio so he could supervise and conduct the singers, or was he just doing an act to qualify for union vocal residuals? When Willie Sutton, a notorious bank robber in the 1930s, was finally arrested, a reporter asked him why he robbed banks. His infamous reply was, "'Cause that's where the money is."

The Halo spot taught me that the real money in the advertising music business did not come from the one-time creative fee, no matter how large, or the one-time arranging fee, no matter how large, or the session fees earned from the AF of M contracts. For an entire generation of composers and arrangers (and their staffs), it came from union *vocal* "resids." *Willie Sutton is alive and well and working on Madison Avenue.*

So I joined the mob. I did what everyone else did—I put my name on the vocal reports whenever I could, sang when it was appropriate, and my income went up accordingly. I hated it. It was dishonest. I had been hired to compose, arrange, and produce; yet singing, or being listed as a singer, was the accepted practice for composers in the industry, and the only way to insure some sort of ongoing income. Sometimes, I would go into the studio and stand with the vocal group, rehearsing them, and then record a first pass, ostensibly to give me something to listen to when I got back in the control booth with my clients. I was a good singer—certainly as good as some—but definitely not at the level of the top talent I wanted to hire to sing the demanding vocal parts I was writing. So I played the game for a while, but then less and less. It was always more important to me to make the track great, and I felt it was not smart business to leave my clients alone in the booth while I *performed* in order to qualify for residuals. Most often, I asked permission to be listed with the hired hands: sometimes I got it, sometimes not.

Advertising agency clients, it turned out, knew all about this practice, and allowed it, the same as they knew about and allowed some of the other perks available to them in the music world. The cost of an exotic on-the-job lunch, or the price of a limo to take the agency producer home after the session— expenses that were unbillable to their clients—could all be buried, padded on to the recording studio invoice as an extra reel of tape. Everyone knew about it; everyone just looked the other way. Some particularly aggressive agency types, who had the ability to squire the music house invoice through their accounting systems, even instructed composers to add a relative's name to the musicians' contract, somewhere in the middle of the string section where it would never be noticed. No one ever actually counted the number of violin players in the room and it was a way for an agency-type to qualify for musicians' residuals. I was never faced with this request, but I know it happened to others.

William Esty Advertising was an ad agency that used lots of music. They had created "Winston Tastes Good Like a Cigarette Should," arguably the most famous cigarette jingle of all time. So busy was their music department that they had a standing booking at A&R Recording Studios each Tuesday and Thursday, blocking off one of the top facilities in New York for their own agency's work. The new cutting-edge sound of my Halo commercial (not my vocal part, of course, but the track that followed it) brought me to the attention of Esty's creative department. My motion picture experience had taught me to compose quickly—I could usually turn out a jingle overnight—and I began doing demos for their new test products. One was for Shakes à la Mode, a packaged powder that you mixed with milk and ice cream to make a shake à la mode. The campaign slogan was "Remember the Alamode!" (I'm not making this up, folks.) Alas, Shakes à la Mode died in test market.

Esty's music director was a holdover from the big-band era, who really didn't understand the new music, and he took the position that anything that he didn't understand was cutting-edge. Once, he asked if I could produce a "Pepper Pot" sound. After listening to his directions for a few moments, I realized that he was talking about the latest Beatles album, *Sgt. Pepper's Lonely Hearts Club Band*. He had probably never heard the album or the song before, but since everyone else was copying the Beatles for advertising, and they were certainly cutting-edge . . . well, you get the rest.

This gentlemen also had a reputation of enjoying three martinis at lunch, something I experienced first-hand one time when I tried to wine-and-dine him. I had to stumble home afterwards to sleep it off. I soon learned from colleagues that the smart way to work with Mr. Martini was to start a session early in the morning, before he showed up, and then be too busy when he wanted to break for lunch. When he came back after lunch, hopefully, you would be finished with everything and ready to announce that he didn't have to hang around because you would send the tapes to the office first thing tomorrow.

I followed "Pepper Pot" with "You Can Take Salem Out of the Country, But . . . " my first network hit for Salem Cigarettes during the years when cigarettes were still allowed to advertise. The creative fee was $2,000, and I signed the standard agency work-for-hire contract, giving up all rights to my song.

But more and more, I was worrying about what would happen if the ad agency decided to use a different jingle house to record rearrangements of my songs, and I no longer had control over which singers' names could appear on the union vocal report.

Then came "Breakaway in a Wide-Tracking Pontiac."

Peter Kelley was the head of the advertising department at the William Morris Agency, a top show-business talent agency, and actively placing Hollywood stars in commercials as spokespersons for major products. Peter was an ingenious promoter: though it was then considered beneath the dignity of a movie actor to appear in a commercial, he had just made a deal for Sir Laurence Olivier to be the on-camera spokesman for Polaroid, and for Arthur Godfrey to appear in spots for a new Proctor and Gamble detergent, Axion. William Morris represented many top Hollywood composers, and Peter wanted to try something different: to represent a cutting-edge advertising composer to the big agencies. For me, it was a golden opportunity to move up the ladder, to have a chance to work for the biggest sponsors while someone else was out there bringing in the jobs. The ten-percent commission was the bargain of a lifetime.

I met with Peter, whom I lovingly and respectfully call "the genius who created my deal," and explained the inner workings of the jingle business, about the twists and curves of the vocal residual and where the income really comes from.

The world was breathlessly awaiting the announcement of the 1969 car-year (as the world breathlessly awaits the announcement of every car-year—if you don't believe me, just ask any car dealer), and Peter put me in touch with Pontiac's ad agency, MacManus, John and Adams, in Detroit. I flew out for a meeting, got my input, and went home to create. A few days later I recorded a demo of "Breakaway in a Wide Trackin' Pontiac." The agency and General Motors client loved the demo so much that they used it as the final on all of their car-year announcement spots.

When it came time for Peter to negotiate the fine points of the financial agreement, I again reminded him of the importance of the vocal residual. He quickly solved the problem: the agency was so thrilled with their new cutting-edge sound that he got them to agree to allow my company to exclusively rearrange all of Pontiac's radio and TV music tracks for that car-year, and to also allow me to be listed as a vocalist on the spots I produced.

Problem solved.

I thought.

Of course, it was a *verbal* agreement, but we all knew that General Motors would never back down on their word.

Hollywood icon Samuel Goldwyn said: "A verbal agreement isn't worth the paper it's written on."

One evening, about halfway through the car-year, I was at home watching TV with my wife and kids and thought I heard something vaguely familiar on one of the commercials. Wait! That's my song, Ma!

It seems that a new producer at MacManus had a wonderful idea: hire Paul Revere and the Raiders to record the second half of the car-year's commercials for Pontiac. Mark Lindsay was the lead singer of this hotter-than-hot cutting-edge rock group, and of course, no one had bothered to tell him or anyone about my verbal exclusivity deal. Where does an 800-pound gorilla sit? Anywhere he likes.

Could I sue Pontiac? I had signed the standard agency music contract and MacManus had the right to do whatever they wanted with my song, including the right *not* to use me as arranger and producer! Or vocalist!

Here's what happened, your Honor . . . Even though I'm not actually singing, sir . . . I am listed as one of the singers on the commercial…it's the industry practice . . . everyone else does it . . . that's where the residuals come from . . .

Young man, let's see if I've got this straight: are you telling this court that you were hired as a composer but you are also being paid as a singer? And you make more money as a singer than as a composer, and you're suing because you're not being paid as a singer when you were hired and paid as a composer? Is that it?

Y . . . y . . . yes, Sir. B . . . b . . . but they p . . . promised!

Ridiculous! Case dismissed!

Even if we were to seriously raise the issue with Pontiac, both William Morris and I would certainly lose the account.

There was nothing to be done.

Peter and I agreed: there had to be a better way.

Chapter 5

The Better Way

This time we got it right.

"Breakaway" had been the car-music hit of 1969, and in 1970, Pontiac asked me to create new music for its next campaign.

Peter Kelley and the MacManus business affairs manager discussed the issue of singing/exclusivity of production. Pontiac clearly did not want to be locked into using one music supplier for an entire year, and we agreed—an advertiser should be free to do whatever it wanted. But, at the same time, though it was the accepted industry practice, we took the position that it wasn't fair to eliminate the composer from all ongoing income from the ongoing uses of his music.

Peter's solution was ingenious: I would create the music, but instead of selling it outright, my company would own and publish the jingle, and give Pontiac an exclusive license to use it in all their advertising for the life of the copyright. In return, the payment would be a standard creative fee, plus the *equiv-*

alent of a residual for every time it was used, whether or not I actually provided the rearrangements.

The agency agreed, reasoning that it was only for a single car-year; and even if the music was used into a second year, their obligation would end as soon as they changed songs, something that American car makers did regularly as they tried to compete with the growing imports from Japan that were clobbering the US car market. In fact, MacManus thought this was such an equitable solution that they had their own lawyer prepare the contract.

The best part for me was that when new ad agencies would call about work, I was able to say that this was the deal that I had with General Motors. It doesn't get better than that! After I explained the fairness of the approach, all my new clients accepted the concept.

I had accomplished the unimaginable—an advertising composer was treated with the same financial respect as a pop songwriter, achieving an ongoing payment for the ongoing uses of his music.

I kept my creative fees in line with the rest of the industry, but so anxious was I to establish the precedent of using my new contract form that I offered to include my *arranging* fees as an advance against the residuals, thereby providing arrange-ments for *free*—also unheard of in the industry—all with the goal of having the agency and client accept my terms.

My existing clients, however, those with whom I had earli-er signed the standard agency give-it-all-away contract, were a problem.

My deal was about to face its biggest test.

Chapter 6

Budweiser—The History of an Account

"YOU CAN LOVE YOUR WIFE, YOU CAN
LOVE YOUR KIDS, YOU CAN LOVE
YOUR COUNTRY, AND YOU CAN
LOVE YOUR DOG. BUT NEVER LOVE
A COMPANY. BECAUSE NO MATTER HOW
MUCH OR HOW LONG YOU LOVE IT,
IT'LL NEVER LOVE YOU BACK."
—Alan J. Tindell, Spokane, Washington

The above quotation paints a painfully accurate portrait of how big business operates: of the investment of passion and spirit that is so willingly offered to a big company by an individual that is then taken for granted and so easily discarded when it serves corporate policy to do so. When you are young, endless enthusiasm overrules all sensibility. In the music business, as you get older, the only way to avoid becoming a victim of the expendability factor is to protect yourself with a copyright and a contract. Mr. Tindell's profound observation puts it all into glaringly clear perspective: in the final analysis, people don't count.

In my novice attempt at PR, I used to send out an announcement on my letterhead to let the advertising community know that I had written a particular new campaign jingle. These one-page mailings, to every client in my address book and every other name in the industry I could find, contained a simple hand-drawn music stave with the notes and slogan of my latest effort—"Chrysler-Plymouth, Comin' Through," "Nationwide Is on Your Side," "Sooner or Later, You'll Own Generals," "At Beneficial (Doot, Doot), You're Good for More"—all followed by "Music, Lyrics, Arrangements, and Production by Steve Karmen."

That was it—a one-liner. Henry Youngman would have been proud.

Once, I sprang for the big bucks to take a quarter-page next to the advertising column in the *New York Times* to announce two new jingles: "Krueger Pilsner Beer," a sponsor of the New York Yankees radio broadcasts that year; and "Devil Shake," a new chocolate drink made by Pepsi Cola. That form of publicity, though momentarily effective and ego-gratifying, proved far too expensive and unnecessary. I decided to let my music speak for itself. You learn as you go.

One day, Bill Fuess, a friendly art director at Ogilvy & Mather Advertising, sent back my latest announcement with some words scribbled on it: "Now all you need is a great beer."

In 1968, I received a phone call from Stu Sherling, a young producer at D'Arcy Advertising in St. Louis. It was one of those pivotal career moments. "Would you like to write for Budweiser?" It was like being asked, "Would you like to play center field for the New York Yankees?"

D'Arcy's new slogan was, "Bud Is the King of Beers, But You Know That . . . ," and, as usual in the jingle industry, it was a creative competition. I don't recall how much the demo fee was except that I added enough to it out of my own pocket to produce the best track I could. In those days, agencies wanted *anthem*-length versions of any new music to begin their client presentations, and composers were told not to worry about the length of the demo. "Just knock their socks off," Stu said.

I wrote a 90-second jingle that did just that: a big-beer rhythm sound, full lyrics, strings, horns, a key change, the works. They loved it! I had won the competition.

At last, after the cars and cigarettes and colas and insurance companies, I had my great beer, Budweiser, the largest-selling beer in the world, the state of the art in its field.

I signed the standard agency music contract, and then watched with pride as my jingle sponsored all the top sporting events that are associated with the King of Beers. The demo became the final, edited down to fit all the 60- and 30-second TV and radio spots that were made that year. I was invited to the annual Anheuser Busch convention in St. Louis, where they introduced *our* new commercials to the assembled cheering beer distributors. Then they introduced me to a Clydesdale. No kidding. There was a long line of bottlers waiting to have their picture taken with one of these giant horses. Talk about people loving their company.

Ed McMahon, Johnny Carson's sidekick on *The Tonight Show*, was Budweiser's on-camera and radio spokesperson, and the agency was pleased to finally have a piece of music that would sound rich and full under his powerful, leathery voice.

The Brewery's marketing strategy was quite sound: find a great song and stick with it, use it in all advertising, radio and TV, either as a lyric version or as background under the copy. (Anheuser Busch was always referred to by its agency as "The Brewery." *The Brewery wants . . . the Brewery doesn't like . . . the Brewery says . . . the Brewery needs . . .*)

Personality-wise, we were a good match. Budweiser projected *pride* in its advertising. The Clydesdale horses brought out a sense of heritage and quality that no other beer has ever been able to match. It takes a certain ego to be the leader, to withstand challenges and still stand tall. Writing for Budweiser appealed to my own sense of pride and I know it showed in my music. "The best for the best," I said to myself in guarded moments of self-satisfaction. To the Brewery, "But You Know That . . . " was a good song; to me, it was the beginning of what I hoped would be a career-long marriage.

Budweiser used the same music tracks for a second year, and my income grew. It was during this time period that I got my "Breakaway Pontiac" education, and began using my new "Peter Kelley" contract.

In 1970, it was time to change songs. Again there was a creative competition. This time D'Arcy's line was: "When You Say Budweiser, You've Said It All." As usual, I wrote all the other lyrics, and invested whatever I thought was necessary to produce the best demo.

On the day of the session we recorded the orchestra tracks first. When the singers arrived to overdub their vocals, I played it for them, singing along, showing them what I wanted. Valerie Simpson would sing the lead, backed up by Kenny Karen, and a big vocal group. Jerry Keller, one of the great singing talents ever in the advertising business, turned to me after the first playback and said, "Don't worry. No one will beat this track."

A few days later, I got a call from Don Sager, the business manager at D'Arcy. They had been dancing in their conference room. I had won the competition. "Would the same deal be OK?"

"No," I said, with forced confidence. "I have a new license form that I've been using with all other clients, and I want to use it here, too." I proceeded to explain the fairness of my deal. He asked that I send him the contract.

The following Friday afternoon (I tend to remember the

days of the week that things happen), Don called to say that the Brewery would not buy my deal.

I asked for the weekend to think it over, perhaps not the response he was expecting.

I knew that they liked my song, but I also knew that they might walk away from it if I didn't give in. I had a young family and we were just beginning on the road to success. Was it worth losing the account and the income it generated? My name had been allowed on the vocal contract for "Bud Is the King of Beers, But You Know That . . . " You can't eat principle, right? Maybe I should just use my new license agreement with clients who were willing to accept it, and sign the standard agency music contract with those who weren't. Maybe I should just keep my mouth shut . . . and sing.

I resisted calling Peter Kelley for advice, afraid that he would say, in typically wise-agent style, "You can't win every battle." Yet, after all the effort it took to devise a fair deal, my instinct wasn't ready to walk away from it simply in the name of "smart business." In retrospect, I've learned that everything is not black and white (I say on these pages that I've learned it—sometimes I'm not sure), and that in the business world there are always ways to resolve differences. Understanding what each side wants and then working toward those goals breeds compromise, without war, without lawyers, and without bloodshed.

Yeah, sure.

At this point, I will respectfully refer you back to Chapter One of this book—"The Mindset of the Author"—about my non-business background and inexperience; about what it takes to be out there on your own all the time; and how that kind of independence often offends those who don't have it. Yes, it may be more prudent to bend when the wind is strong against you, but I wanted to be the best at what I did—the same as Budweiser—and I worked hard at it; and that kind of effort generates a special energy and passion that is only available from someone who works for himself, and not as an employee on some else's payroll. And you can't get it from a person who will sign any document placed in front of him just because someone declares that it's a *standard agreement*.

It costs more.

And it's worth it.

To cut a long philosophical dissertation short, I decided to give in. The practical issues far outweighed the emotional ones. I was no longer the kid who had just quit school to go on the road and make music. I had responsibilities to people besides myself.

It was a horrible weekend. I'd like to describe it as a rainy and dark. That's how my soul felt. That's what it feels like now as I write these words.

On Monday morning, the phone rang.

Someone up there was watching out for me.

It was D'Arcy's business manager. "Good morning, Steve. This is Don. They bought your deal."

Peter Bart, the editor in chief of *Variety*, has written, "You don't get what's fair, you get what you negotiate." I've often wondered what my life would have been like if they hadn't given in. Or if they hadn't called me first. But, from that moment on, I realized that I was only as good as my song: if they wanted it, it was worthy of a fair contract; if they hadn't thought it was good enough, it would not have mattered what kind of a deal we made.

I never worked without my contract again.

It was the beginning of a heady time.

In my naïvety, I began to feel like I was "part of the great Brewery family," and it showed in my work.

"When You Say Bud . . . " won the Clio Award that year for best music and lyrics. I began producing all different styles of rearrangements for radio. Each one was a bigger hit than the previous. I had used a tuba on the original demo, and the "Tuba Track" was featured on every Budweiser TV commercial, with no signs of getting old.

I gave a license to Hal Leonard Music to print a marching band arrangement of "When You Say Bud . . . " and the Brewery mailed out thousands of copies to universities all over America. As a result, college bands began to play the jingle, increasing its popularity. At the University of Wisconsin they sang a slightly amended lyric—"When You Say *Wisconsin*, You've Said It All"—every time the Badgers scored a touchdown. But soon, the huge crowds were forbidden from singing during the game: their foot-stamping enthusiasm was literally shaking the foundations of the stadium. Today, the singing is still a tradition, but for safety reasons only allowed at the end of each game.

August Busch III had just taken over the reins of Anheuser Busch from his father, "Gussy" Busch, and was determined to expand the company and build breweries all across America. The bigger they got, the more they advertised.

In a moment of typical agency farsightedness (or nervousness), D'Arcy called and asked if I could come up with some ideas for a follow-up campaign, to be used in case "When You Say Bud . . . " needed replacing. "Everything is fine, everyone is happy beyond words. We'd just like to hear some new thinking, to keep on the back burner. Spend whatever you have to on demos. This is all exploratory, you know, just in case . . . "

I was "part of the family," and would do anything necessary.

A few weeks later, I flew out to St. Louis, and presented "Here Comes the King." There was no place for it in the regular Budweiser advertising, but they liked it so much that it became the Clydesdale theme. I recorded a special Christmas version for a TV spot that showed a team of eight horses trotting through the snow. No announcer. Just music. That beautiful commercial ran for twenty-five years. When the beer wars erupted in the late 1970s, Miller Beer also produced a Christmas spot, of a single horse pulling a sled through the snow. Miller licensed the rights to "I'll Be Home for Christmas" as their music-under theme. The public was never aware that Miller's single horse was Silky Sullivan, one of the all-time champion pacers.

One horse was no match for eight Clydesdales. Nor was Miller's licensed pop song any match for Budweiser's original music. Each year, America marked the start of the Christmas season when those eight Clydesdales came trotting through the snow.

Michelob was Anheuser Busch's super premium beer, then available only in regional areas and in taverns. When it went national, I wrote "The Michelob Drinking Song—Surprise People with the Unexpected Pleasure of Michelob."

We followed that campaign with "Weekends Were Made for Michelob."

Next, "When Do You Say Budweiser?" became the companion jingle for "When You Say Bud, You've Said It All."

In 1973, my wife died of colon cancer (Sandy was thirty-five), and the Brewery was generously understanding about my work schedule. It took time to reorganize my life, to involve myself in school schedules, to take care of my three young daughters, but when I finally thought I was ready to come back to work, I couldn't concentrate. I had lost my spirit, my passion. Nothing seemed important except my kids. Budweiser had a new TV commercial called "Hot Dogger," and the film sat on my desk waiting for me to do an arrangement. I still couldn't do it. They had a deadline. It would have been the first time in five years that someone else would be writing a Budweiser spot.

I called D'Arcy and stalled. They waited until they could not wait any longer. It was one of those defining moments again. I agreed to try. It was the most difficult arrangement I had ever done. Not difficult in its musicality, but in breaking out of the malaise that was gripping my world. I knew I had to go back to work.

Someone up there was watching out for me.

"Hot Dogger" won the Clio for the best rearrangement of that year.

On the business side, I was feeling more and more a part of the Brewery family. We signed a new contract for every new song—*my* standard form license agreement.

When I received calls for potential jobs from other clients, I always sent my contract form to them first, along with a bid letter, before I started work on the demo. If they didn't agree to my deal, I didn't do the job. I walked away from some enormous creative fees simply because the sponsor wanted to own the copyright. Every new client, without exception, accepted my deal.

One holdover from my pre-smart days was Nationwide Insurance. In 1967, I had signed the Ogilvy & Mather standard agency music contract for "Nationwide Is on Your Side," and they owned it. Each year, they always asked me to write the rearrangements for their new TV spots, but I was not allowed a vocal residual, or even the chance to sing. Ogilvy stuck to its guns, even though they later accepted my contract for "Hershey Is the Great American Chocolate Bar." Trying to redo an old deal is very difficult, something I was about to learn in spades. One year, I refused to do the Nationwide rearrangements unless they agreed to some sort of ongoing payment for uses of those new arrangements. They hired someone else. I never worked for Nationwide again. As I write this, after thirty-five years of passing through several different advertising agencies, "Nationwide Is on Your Side" is still on the air bringing in income to others. It stands as my shining reminder of what might have been if I had not achieved a fair deal for the continuing uses of my other compositions.

There were a few times when I didn't win an account for an agency I represented in a new business pitch—other agencies had better strategies—but one-on-one against colleagues I had never lost a competition.

In the industry, I had become the composer of last resort. When an agency couldn't get what they wanted from someone else, they agreed to my deal and I got the job done for them. If it was pro bono work, I eliminated the creative and arranging fees, but we always signed a contract. And I always carefully filed for a copyright on every new jingle as well as for each new rearrangement. I became more familiar with agency business managers and their lawyers than any composer in the industry. "I won't change a word, so let's not waste time," was my standard response. Then I would refer them to a business manager at another agency so they might learn that my deal worked well for both sides. No one balked. I was the living example of the American dream: I provided a good product that someone wanted, and charged accordingly.

Again, to be very clear, my creative and arranging fees never exceeded what others jingle houses were charging. And for many years I included the incentive of arranging fees as an advance against residuals. I just did it differently, with my own contract form.

In 1976, the copywriters at D'Arcy came up with an idea for a Michelob TV spot that showed an orchestra conductor leading an outdoor summer concert. When they asked me to do the arrangement, I asked who they had in mind to play the conductor.

It wasn't me.

I wasn't happy. "I'm a conductor, why not?"

"We want someone who looks seriously like a conductor."

"OK, get your serious conductor to do the chart."

They gave in.

"I don't act for scale, you know," I joked.

They weren't sure I was joking, so I pushed the envelope again—we agreed on scale plus $1. The extra buck was for the pride I knew they could get nowhere else.

We spent ten hours—from 6 PM until 4 AM—in the blistering summer heat in a band shell out in rural New Jersey. Over and over the orchestra played along with the pre-recorded version of my new symphonic arrangement of "Weekends Were Made for Michelob," while the crew concentrated on beer-pouring shots. The top studio musicians in New York had agreed to appear on-camera so they could earn actor-amount residuals, and when I suggested to the film director that they were wilting in the merciless 100-degree heat, he reminded me: "There's beer in the spot, too, Steve."

A necessary touch of humility.

Weekend Pops was broadcast for the first time in 1977 on the television show of Elvis Presley's last concert—Elvis had died just a few weeks earlier—and won a Clio Award later that year for the best rearrangement of an existing theme.

I was working my tail off for the Brewery trying to keep all their beers creatively different: using different styles of orchestrations and different vocal approaches for each brand; traveling back and forth from coast to coast, recording Lou Rawls in Los Angeles for Budweiser; Brook Benton in New York for Michelob; doing demos—for free—and developing new songs for Bud and Michelob—for free. Once, I had to ask my life-long friend Connie Francis to intervene with Tony Bennett who had refused to perform overdubs on a session for Michelob because he insisted on recording live, which for that job was impossible. There were nine separate television tracks to record-to-picture and Tony would have had to stand around all day waiting to sing one line at the end of each spot— "Weekends Were Made for Michelob"—while my client made the usual on-session adjustments. (Tony didn't get the job—

they gave it to Vic Damone.)

Word got back to me that the Brewery didn't like the fact that I had written music for Colt .45 Malt Liquor ("A Completely Unique Experience"), National Bohemian Beer ("The Land of Pleasant Living"), and Olympia Beer ("Oly-Oly-Oh"), all regional beers. I had no contract of exclusivity with Anheuser Busch, but I ended my relationship with these other companies anyway. Why not? I was "part of the family," right?

The Brewery's business was expanding and I was keeping up. Miller had introduced Miller Lite and now every brewer wanted to capture a part of the exploding light beer market. "Won't Fill You Up, Won't Let You Down" was the campaign for "Anheuser Light," the Brewery's first light beer. "The First Malt Liquor Good Enough to Be Called Budweiser" brought the Brewery charging into the market previously dominated by Colt .45.

We conducted the search for "Lower and Deeper." Miller's Lowenbrau Beer was using Arthur Prysock as their singer. Mr. Prysock has one of the great deeeeeeeep voices of all time, and his "Let It Be Lowenbrauuuuuuuu" performance at the end of each spot not only scraped the floor in perfect pitch, but was also being imitated by comedians across America. The Brewery wanted to find an even deeeeeeeeeeeeeeper voice.

We auditioned jazz great Johnny Hartman, pop great Johnny Desmond, studio singers Milt Grayson and Mike Stewart, each of whom could sing low Cs in their sleep. Finally, after calling agents and managers for ideas, the Brewery agreed: the immortal Billy Eckstine—"Mr. B."—sang "Good Taste Runs in the Family," to introduce Michelob Light.

I had been the Brewery's only composer for ten years. There were new faces at D'Arcy; new producers, art directors, account people, and they were usually sent to my recording sessions with strict instructions to "monitor" but not interfere.

In retrospect, the business side of me should have been content with all that work, but I wanted to feel even more a part of a family. I was turning down other clients to be constantly available to handle the Brewery's ever-growing business.

Looking back at those turbulent times, I see a young composer caught in throes of a classic dilemma. I guess I was worn down from all the juggling and my artistic side was feeling unappreciated. All their singing stars were earning double scale payments, while I was endlessly piecing together vocal tracks to make one complete acceptable performance. In advertising, it's not the performer; it's the song, right? But, they were giving more respect to the singer. This was not the record business. In advertising, the song is king, right?

I sought a vote of confidence.

Was my bravado—or insecurity—being influenced by other factors in my life? I was a single parent with three daughters entering their teenage years. Any parent understands what that feels like. Was I subconsciously angry that I had to raise three kids by myself and run a business at the same time? That anger had to go somewhere. I had no one to seek advice from, not that I would have listened anyway. But when my wife was alive we had talked things over, and there was a calming voice of reason in my world.

This time I was on my own.

I asked for a raise.

D'Arcy sent business manager Don Sager to meet with me. We talked for two days. When he left I felt that someone was finally clear about what it took to do all that work.

Was I ever wrong.

I thought of the old adage, "Familiarity breeds contempt."

Don called a few days later to say that the Brewery had refused my request for a raise in residuals.

What should I do? What does any employee do when he asks for a raise and is then refused? My experiences as a soda jerk and bookstamper were of no use here. Should I suck it up and continue on the job? Did they care? Would we ever look at each other in the same way again? Was there ever a "we?"

Or should I walk? I had the protection of my contracts. My company would be paid for the uses of my music whether I provided the rearrangements or not.

Sometimes you go to the well once too often.

I decided to resign their business.

Not that I was wrong in doing what I did. I just did it the wrong way.

I had clearly lost focus that this was only a *business* relationship, and nothing more, a very dangerous thing to do. Family? I was about to learn that I was as expendable to Anheuser Busch as an old beer can.

I've written three or four really stupid letters in my lifetime, letters that I would greatly like to retract. I guess everyone has a few of those. What I needed to say could have been accomplished in one business-like sentence, something like: "I deeply regret that, under current circumstances, I am unable to continue to produce music for Anheuser Busch." That would have been smart.

Instead, my wounded ego and pride overruled any good sense. They had said "no" to me. I composed one of those "Do you know how valuable I am to you, no one has ever done more for you than *me*," four-page single-spaced missives, and sent it not only to D'Arcy, but to the brand manager at Anheuser Busch, as well as August Busch himself.

A few days later, Don Sager called to tell me that they were moving on and had given the next package of Budweiser commercials to someone else.

An amazing thing happened: Budweiser did not go out of business. Hard to believe, isn't it?

Well, maybe the Brewery would soften, I thought. OK, I was the black sheep in the family who had gotten out of line and needed a little kid-glove treatment. A little forgiveness. Maybe they would change their minds.

Yeah, sure.

After a while, colleagues began to call, asking what had happened. I ducked the subject. This was a family fight, and no one's business. One old-time jingle house owner called and wanted my permission "to go after the Budweiser business." It was as though the circling sharks could smell blood in the water. I told him he didn't need my permission. He was someone with a reputation of being willing to screw his mother if it meant getting a job. When I hung up, I really got mad, and wrote *him* a letter, telling him just that. After a few months of blazing correspondence back and forth, I apologized.

I was hurt, and the pain was all of my own making.

Could it have worked out differently? In the real world, after ten great years, it was natural for the new agency faces at D'Arcy to want to work with other music houses. The music business was changing. Wasn't the whole concept of my contract to provide security when others rearranged my songs? I was being paid anyway, right?

Yes, but I missed Budweiser terribly. I thought of how Babe Ruth must have felt when the Yankees found it convenient to trade him away to the Boston Braves at the end of his career.

To be sure, my career was not ending. I was in my prime, as busy as ever working on other projects. "Ford, That's Incredible," "Trust the Midas Touch," "Exxon-Energy for a Strong America," "America Believes in Liberty Mutual Insurance," "Don't Say Drug Store, Say Drug Fair," "Aren't You Glad You Use Dial," "Wrigley Spearmint Gum, Gum Gum . . . ," "A Taste of Europe—TWA," "You Can't Beat the Experience—Pan Am," "Hertz, We're America's Wheels," were all giant campaign songs that represented those products for many years. And each year, at "car time," I wrote something new for Pontiac, or Cadillac, or Dodge, or Chrysler.

In 1977, "I Love New York" became the very first tourism campaign ever sponsored by a state government. In 1980, it was proclaimed as the official state song of New York State. My music was now enshrined with some pretty exclusive company: "My Old Kentucky Home," "Maryland, My Maryland," "Georgia on My Mind"; composers Stephen Foster, Hoagy Carmichael. I was one of only fifty, a most magnificent career honor. I had come a long way from the porno movie scores.

The beer wars were really raging. Miller Beer, recently purchased by Kraft Foods, had begun a new campaign to capture the what-do-you-do-after-work market using the slogan "It's Miller Time." In response, D'Arcy changed the lyrics of "When You Say Budweiser, You've Said It All" to "For All You Do, This Bud's for You," and, wanting to out-clout Miller, hired almost every rock group in America to record a version. Though I was not involved in any production, thanks to my contract my income grew accordingly.

They didn't like that.

In 1980, in a moment of wanting to express regret— remorse, wisdom, there is no correct word—I called Anheuser Busch's marketing manager, Mike Roarty, and asked if he would have dinner with me. I flew to St. Louis, met him at a restaurant, and apologized for my letter and my impetuous anger. We parted as friends, and I was hopeful that at some point I would be given the opportunity to rejoin "the family."

Then D'Arcy got into trouble. Up until then, all of the Brewery's national beer advertising had been produced by that one agency. In fact, August Busch's cousin was the CEO of D'Arcy, which probably helped their relationship a lot. But the beer world was growing, and now every brewer had a premium brand, a super-premium, a light beer, a dark beer, and a malt liquor. Anheuser Busch wanted to hear new ideas and new thinking for *everything*. Remember "There's no such thing as loyalty"? It works on the agency side of the street, too.

Initially, D'Arcy had created its own problems. Michelob changed campaigns from "Weekends Were Made for Michelob," to "Put a Little Weekend in Your Week," which effectively shortened the life of that unique positioning. Soon, other agencies were competing for that brand.

In 1981, I received a call from Don Sager, still the business manager at D'Arcy.

Anheuser Light and Natural Light had each done fairly well against the category leader, Miller Lite. (There was even a lawsuit about the spelling of "Light"/"Lite"—Miller claimed that no other beer could use the word "Light"—Miller lost.) But now, the Brewery had decided to put their flagship name on a light beer. "Budweiser Light" was about to enter the market, and the Brewery would not settle for anything less than a hit. Much to D'Arcy's dismay, another agency was allowed to make a creative pitch for the business.

DDB Needham in Chicago, working on spec, had created a terrific campaign for the new Bud Light entitled, "Bring Out Your Best." Not only did they film three great TV spots at their own expense, but had a great song written by Gary Klaff and Mark Weinstein, two of Chicago's top composers. Don sent me a video of the commercials. One spot showed an older hockey player—the goalie—being challenged by one of the rookies. "Bring out your best!" screams the rock singer, as the young player skates towards the net. "Bring out your best," screams the vocal again, as the old pro reaches down inside himself for that last drop of energy, strength, spirit, and pride (all those things that beer guys respond to). The kid takes the shot, the old guy stops the puck, and they both smile at each other and go out to have a beer. We hear "Bring out your best" once more as they pour a Bud Light.

Solid strategy. Great execution. Wonderful music. The other spots were about football and baseball. It would take a miracle to beat this first-class effort.

Don asked if I would be willing to help develop a jingle that might save the account for D'Arcy. The Brewery was not told that I had been consulted—Don assured me that any ruffled feathers would be smoothed over later if we won. They had gone to several other music houses, and not liked the result. I was their composer of last resort. I flew to St. Louis, and immediately, but unintentionally, put the creative team on the defensive by expressing admiration for the "Bring Out Your Best" spots. The whole place reeked of desperation, so different from the solid confidence I had felt there years earlier. D'Arcy's Bud Light strategy was to have an old Clydesdale horse run alongside a young Clydesdale, accompanied by a song extolling the pride and heritage of the new brand. They had been selling pride effectively for years, but it was not hard to see why the "Bring Out Your Best" spots stood out: they talked about real people, and there was a new audience who wanted more than horses.

I wrote something that I thought answered their needs, and made a presentation by phone to a room full of depressed, underwhelmed people. They didn't like it enough to even authorize a real demo. A few days later I learned that D'Arcy had lost the account.

But Budweiser's "This Bud's for You" was running stronger than ever.

By 1985, D'Arcy Advertising had already merged into D'Arcy, MacManus, John and Adams Advertising; then into D'Arcy, MacManus and Masius Advertising; then into D'Arcy, Masius, Benton and Bowles Advertising; and then into DMB&B, joining the alphabet crowd. Although this corporate entity still represented Budweiser from its office in St. Louis, most of the people from my era were gone.

Once again, Don Sager called, this time to advise me that Budweiser was going to announce a new worker-salute campaign. "When You Say Bud"/"This Bud's for You" had been on the air continuously for over fifteen years, and now "You Make America Work, and This Bud's for You," was going to replace it. More to the point, he had been instructed to inform me that D'Arcy's lawyers had thoroughly examined their legal position, and that their "new music" constituted a brand new song, which would no longer require payments under our existing contract. He sent me a tape.

Quite typically, the beginning of their song was different. This happens often with long-running campaigns that want to say something new, but then come back to the classic logo that marries the new idea to the old. In this case, after all the exposition of their new selling strategy "You Make America Work . . . . " they came back to the same musical logo that had been used for years, "This Bud's for You." Instead of the notes 6-4-2-1, they made it 4-3-2-1. The rhythm figure was exactly the same.

"If it weren't for my song, there could never have been their song," I said to Don. "The ending of the 'new' song is nothing more than a rearrangement of my song, not unlike the hundreds of ad lib versions that had been done through the years. If the Brewery doesn't accept that position, I will enforce my contract legally."

I didn't hear from anyone for a few months. Then the other shoe fell.

I was returning from a vacation with my kids, and called my office from the airport. Anheuser Busch had just served us with papers, suing my company, asking for a declaratory judgment that their song was indeed completely original, and therefore that no payments were required under the terms of our contract. We had to respond before a judge within three days.

I called my attorney. Two days later we were in federal court.

write this next section with a little wry smile. You see, I'm a
believer in the theory that things are meant to be when they
are meant to be, and that events happen for a reason.

The judge assigned to the case was named Robert Ward, a
man of about fifty. When we entered the courtroom, he was
loudly ruling from the bench on another matter, dictating his
opinion right there in open court. Bam bam bam, strong and
solid in his thoughts. When he got to us, the first thing he said
to Budweiser's attorney and mine was, "I know all about beer
commercials. I watch football every Sunday, and I know what's
going on. When are you going to be ready for trial?" My attorney and I conferenced: this judge was someone who certainly
knew my song, a fact that would help us enormously. "We are
ready now," my attorney answered, displaying a confidence
that caught Budweiser's attorney off guard.

"Well, not today!" the judge laughed. He agreed to fast-
track the case.

What followed was two months of 24/7 preparation for trial.
Days, nights, weekends, depositions, document production,
the works. Budweiser had hired Skadden Arps Meager &
Flom, one of the major legal firms in the world, plus a second
copyright-specialist, plus their own in-house counsel, plus a
topflight musicologist. We had a musicologist of our own, and
were counting on the Judge Ward's familiarity with the advertising to work for our side.

The defendant in these kinds of cases is usually given the
choice of whether to have the matter heard before a jury, or
just a judge. We chose Judge Ward, for obvious reasons: whatever Budweiser's attorney could present might be equalized by
the familiarity that he had after fifteen years of hearing my
song. It was certainly worth the shot.

Three days before the trial date, we received notice that
Judge Ward had been called away on another matter, and that
we would now have a *senior* judge to hear our case. We looked

his name up in the Goggle of the time: Judge Edmund Lumbard was a highly respected jurist who was also, unfortunately, eighty-five years old.

The facts of a case that could hinge on the subtle musical differences between 6-4-2-1 and 4-3-2-1 were now going to be decided by an eighty-five-year-old judge who quite likely never watched television, certainly not the kind of sporting events that Budweiser sponsored.

And, on top of it all, he was hard of hearing.

When the trial began and I was called to testify, my attorney instructed me to speak loudly. Each day, Judge Lumbard sat high up on his bench, paying attention with his hands cupped about his ears. We kept our music playbacks loud, too.

Budweiser's musicologist presented a series of highly technical comparisons of songs, all projected in color on a large screen. Our musicologist argued that there may be differences of nuance in the *courtroom*, but the songs were surely perceived the same in America's *living room*, and that's what counted in advertising. My song gave Budweiser a continuity that could not be denied.

Well, that's what we thought, anyway.

The trial lasted six days.

Judge Lumbard's ruling came a month later.

We lost.

I had the option to appeal.

I sent Budweiser's lawyer a letter congratulating him on his victory and advising him that I would not appeal.

It took too much of my soul to continue that fight.

It had cost me $237,500 to get that far. You don't forget a number like that—$237,500 for legal fees. I had fought the good fight, big-time lawyers, and lost. I was later told that Anheuser Busch had spent more than $2 million on their own legal fees.

It was over.

Their new campaign went on the air, and ran only for a

year, though the slogan "This Bud's for You," continues to be the industry-leading banner for Budweiser.

The residuals stopped.

Another of the "fringe benefits" of self-employment.

There is a happy ending to this story. At least a happ*ier* ending.

My timeless Christmas-Clydesdale spot continued to run until just a few years ago, when commercials of horses-playing-football took over, and Super Bowl mentality began replacing any sense of heritage. Perhaps it will be brought back someday. There should be a place for something memorable in the grand Budweiser picture.

I've come to recognize that the problems that developed through the years of my relationship with the Brewery were mostly of my own making: of my need to feel like a *part of the family*, something that for a vendor is impossible to achieve and a big mistake to desire. Advertising is a temporary business, and anyone who thinks that his creation will go on forever is naïve. However, it is the artist's job to protect his work as best he can so he can participate in its successes when it is used, whether the current system likes it or not. I accomplished that, and have no complaints. My songs have outlasted everyone that was around when they began.

I am also long beyond any anger about their lawsuit. In some ways I feel sorry for this great brand. I've watched Budweiser advertising go from memorable music, to frogs and lizards talking in a swamp, to frat-house comedy, to farting horses. Oh, was the flatulent horse for Bud *Light*? Sorry, I couldn't tell the difference between marketing strategies. The Clydesdales are still a magnificent unique image, but one-liner jokes seem to appeal to the vast impermanence that everyone covets today: like them or not, the ads are part of our culture. There's a new cutting-edge out there, and it slices any which way it wants.

In 1998, twenty-eight years after I wrote "When You Say Budweiser, You've Said It All," I sent a notice to the Brewery's legal department advising them that their license to use the song during the first term of the copyright would expire at the end of that year. This was a formality—it wasn't part of their advertising anyway. But it also meant they could no longer broadcast their famous "This Bud's for You" song without renegotiating. Our 1970 contract did not call for a renewal into the second term of the copyright. (In contrast, the "Here Comes the King," contract did provide for use during all copyright renewals.)

Shortly thereafter, I received a call from the Budweiser account supervisor at Anheuser Busch. D'Arcy Advertising was long gone, and Budweiser's commercials were now being produced by several different ad agencies. This very polite gentleman, from a younger generation, was extremely complimentary about the *passion* he heard in my music that seemed unavailable anywhere else. I told him that I was no longer active in the advertising business, but he asked if I would be willing to come to St. Louis to meet with him. He said he had no knowledge of Budweiser's law suit against me, and that he would simply like to get to know me.

Yeah, sure.

He met me at the airport with a limo, and first took me to the Anheuser Busch Visitors Center, where he gave me the full dog-and-pony-show tour. As we walked through the great hall, filled with exhibits of racing cars, antique horse carriages, and every imaginable kind of garment all emblazoned with Anheuser Busch–brand logos, I could hear my music blaring out over the loudspeaker system. Every song I had every written for the Brewery—"Bud Is the King of Beers, But You Know That," "When You Say Budweiser, You've Said It All," "When Do You Say Budweiser?," "Here Comes the King," "This Bud's for You," "Weekends Were Made for Michelob"—

was playing everywhere, in the factory where they make bottles, in the rooms where they brewed the beer, and in the hallways. There was a photographer waiting to take my picture with a really big Clydesdale. Then, we had lunch in the corporate dining room, and when we finally sat in the privacy of his office, I tried to lead the conversation:

"I have no desire to start any kind of war about the copyright renewal, and I think that this might be an appropriate time for me to sell back to you all of the songs that I have ever composed for Anheuser Busch." We agreed that I would make a written proposal. He had the limo take me back to the airport.

I am not permitted to disclose the terms of transfer, but I didn't kill them, nor did they kill me. We reached a fair ending to a three decade, often contentious relationship.

The only bump came when they sent me the document that would transfer the copyrights. It had been prepared by their legal department and was completely one-sided in its terms, and ignored the new spirit of friendship that I felt had been rekindled, at least for that brief moment. (See, here I go again, thinking that there can be a friendship with a giant corporation.) When I complained about the tone of the contract, I was told by their lawyer that it was the only agreement they would use. I suggested to them that if we could not agree on satisfactory language, then we would have no deal, and having made a good-faith offer I would then feel free to sell my copyrights on the open market. "If this deal falls apart based on a disagreement about wording, I'll sell the music to Miller," I said.

Silence.

They really didn't like *that*.

I drew up my own agreement, without the assistance of a lawyer, made sure they indemnified me for all new uses of the songs after the sale—their contract had me offering a ridiculous unlimited indemnification for all future uses of a song that I had written twenty-eight years ago—and sent it to them.

It was a done deal.

This time for an ending, not a beginning.

It was a relationship for which I can only be grateful.

It's worth repeating Mr. Tindell's words here:

"YOU CAN LOVE YOUR WIFE, YOU CAN LOVE YOUR KIDS, YOU CAN LOVE YOUR COUNTRY, AND YOU CAN LOVE YOUR DOG. BUT NEVER LOVE A COMPANY. BECAUSE NO MATTER HOW MUCH OR HOW LONG YOU LOVE IT, IT'LL NEVER LOVE YOU BACK."

Chapter 7

The Enemy Was Us

The drug of vocal residuals was irresistible. Jingle composers were happy to sign the standard agency music contract and give up all rights to the future uses of their works in return for a one-time creative fee. As long as they could sing, they thought they were safe. Vocal residuals were a painless ongoing payment—no one had to negotiate with the agency business manager or fight with the agency lawyer—and no one complained. To be listed as a union vocalist became the ultimate industry goal. A person wishing to join the musicians' union had to pass a test to prove they could actually play an instrument; but people who could barely carry a tune could not be refused membership in AFTRA and SAG as long as they had a legitimate job offer from a union-signatory company. Every jingle house, of course, was, or became, a union-signatory company.

By the mid 1970s, the first multi-track tape machines had evolved from the four-track miracle that had revolutionized the business, to eight-track; to sixteen-track; and then to twenty-four-track. Each was considered the state-of-the-art for about fifteen minutes. Some studios offered the ability to lock two twenty-four-track machines together in sync, thereby providing the astounding flexibility of forty-eight-track recording. Jingle composers and their audio engineers began to hold strategy conferences before sessions to map out the track *split*. Individual instruments or sections of instruments were assigned their own separate home, where audio effects could be added—compression, equalization, echo, delay—all without *leaking* on to any other instrument's track. Drums were assigned five or six tracks (snare, bass drum, hi-hat, left cymbals, right cymbals, overhead); the bass had a track, as did the trumpets, woodwinds, tenor trombones, and bass trombone; the piano could be recorded in stereo with two microphones on two tracks; violins, violas, and celli were each kept *discrete*; timpani, vibes, tambourines, conga drums, finger bells—anything the arranger required—could all be recorded separately, and/or added later at the whim of the jingle producer.

Regardless of how many tracks were available on the tape, there were never enough to satisfy the growing imaginations of composers and arrangers; or the uncertainty of an agency producer who couldn't make up his mind, and now used the technology to record an *alternate* version and delay a final decision until later. A session that was once done *live*, and considered finished when the actual performance was perfected, had evolved into a vast musical jigsaw puzzle where each individual piece was first constructed, tweaked, and polished, and then assembled later into a final version called the *mix*. "We'll fix it in the mix," became the mantra of the era. Studio costs for all that separate recording time, plus all that extra mixing time, were soaring. But, no matter the size of the orchestra, there were always at least six or eight tracks left open for the all-important *vocal* overdubs.

A new expression was being heard on every jingle session: "Let's *double* it." The use of this phrase gave birth to a whole other level of problems for the advertising industry, and was to have a far greater negative effect than anyone could foresee on the long-term health of the jingle business.

Doubling meant that if five singers (for example) sang a track and then overdubbed themselves—performing exactly the same parts a second time on a separate track (*"doubling it"*)—it created a different effect than if ten singers had sung only once. Jingle producers took the position that this was the new cutting-edge sound that their clients wanted. If the voices were tripled, the sound got even better. Harmony parts were added separately on a fourth, fifth, and sixth tracks—as many as it took to get "the sound." Doubling became the rage. Phil Specter's infamous Wall of Sound was made possible by the technology that allowed the doubling of the same vocal group again and again.

The ability to *double* hid many sins. It didn't matter if the singers were top caliber, although no jingle producer would ever admit that a professional vocalist had a better voice than the musical arranger or the office bookkeeper. If the first vocal layer had a few clams, or was a little flat, a double could cure it. The Chipmunks could sound like the Mormon Tabernacle Choir after a *triple*. Jingle producers always carefully covered up any inadequacies in their home-grown vocal performances by booking a few ringers, two or three really good professional jingle singers, who would carry the heavyweight lead parts while still allowing the usual suspects to be listed on the union vocal contract. One professional jingle singer told me that she often stood in a vocal group next to people from the jingle house that she had never seen before, "who were merely just moving their mouths."

The craft unions, always the last to acknowledge advancing technology, took differing stances to defend their members as the industry roared into the age of multi-tracking.

The AF of M initially viewed overdubbing as illegal, in violation of the collective bargaining agreements between the agencies and the union. *Music was meant to be played* live, *all at once, not in parts to be assembled later*. But illegal or not, overdubbing was reality.

Players, wanting their piece of the new hi-tech pie, had begun to report to their union about all the overdubbing that was going on in the studios. The union announced that if a musician's recorded track was used as a background for a new recording (either an instrumental *sweetening* or a vocal overdub), then *all* the musicians in the basic band must continue to be paid as if they were still in the room, playing. That meant if a music session took an hour and the vocal overdub took a second hour, all the players had to be paid two hours of scale payments, even though they had only been in the room working for a single hour.

Budgets were bulging, but jingle producers blamed technology. Because of overdubbing, the names of the composer, arranger, producer, and all other jingle house faces who were traditionally listed on the musicians' contract were now earning larger session fees, larger pension contributions, and better medical coverage. Overdubbing was definitely to everyone's benefit.

At first, the advertising agencies instructed jingle producers to delay the vocal overdubs until all the musicians had left the building, hoping to hide what they were doing. This, of course, was futile—everyone knew anyway. Then, the AF of M tried sending representatives to monitor recording sessions, and began requiring jingle producers to give forty-eight-hour notice prior to the start of a date so they could assign a delegate to attend. This didn't work either. Using the "I forgot" or "the job only came in last night" response, jingle producers were able to avoid the unpleasantness of a cigar-smoking union delegate standing around in the studio while they worked. Sometimes, jingle producers would lock the studio doors if they heard that a delegate was in the building while an illegal vocal overdub was taking place.

Ultimately, the AF of M could do little more than complain: ever fearful of offending their jingle-house employers, no player was willing to let his name be used if the union wanted to bring an offending company up on formal charges. There was just a lot of *warning*. Later, jingle producers (with the reluctant permission of the advertisers) began to pay a token *twenty minutes extra* to the orchestra members for each spot that was overdubbed, no matter how long it actually took, and this seemed to calm the AF of M, even though it was still against the written code. The twenty-minutes-extra concept was eventually dropped because it was unenforceable, and musicians' scale payments have remained exactly that ever since: just scale.

For singers, the financial consequences of doubling were huge. AFTRA and SAG took the position that when a group of five vocalists (for example) sang a basic layer, and doubled themselves five times to get "the sound," they were, in effect, *twenty-five* people, and each singer should each be paid *five times* the scale session-fee payment. The new technology, from the union's historical point of view, was putting twenty people out of work. Initially, the agencies accepted this logic.

The biggest differences, however, were how each union viewed *residual* payments for their members. For musicians, no matter how many hours of session-fee payment it took to complete one commercial, the spot was still considered only one commercial for residuals. But, for the singers who had performed five times on one commercial, it meant *five times* residuals, too. It didn't matter if a group sang a whole song or just one word: they were paid *five times* network Class-A residual scale, plus *five times* regional scale, plus *five times* pension contributions, plus *five times* EVERYTHING!

One particularly enterprising jingle composer pushed avarice to undreamed-of heights: overdubbing a vocal group *eight times* (of course, he was an indispensable member of the group), and getting the agency to pay it! It's worth noting that the vocal scales per singer in a group of "three to five" singers—a union designation—are higher than for a group of "six to eight" singers, thereby providing composer/producers with yet another incentive to have a smaller group do more overdubs.

An old-time agency producer smiled as he recalled the initial outcry: "The first time we saw the music estimates, we couldn't believe it: a thirteen-week residual cycle for a twenty-piece band was $1,640. The vocal residuals for five singers were $34,000!"

Unlike the musicians' union, which caved in to the technology, a sweet working compromise was reached with AFTRA and SAG: a vocalist who *doubled* would receive fifty percent over scale, and that extra amount would also cover all unlimited subsequent overdubs. Scale had automatically become scale-and-a-half because everyone was doubling to create "the sound." And, for singers, the fifty percent more concept applied to *residuals* as well!

As jingle producers became greedier, every commercial had a vocal group on it, whether needed or not. The artistic argument was persuasive: wouldn't the sponsor like to have the name of his product sung by a big group instead of just one voice, giving it that big, cutting-edge sound, and making it more memorable to the consumer? (*Doubled*, of course.) The agencies all worked on commission: if the client was willing to pay, why not? True, the spot really calls for a solo voice, but wouldn't it sound fuller with a little "oooh-aaah" vocal group in the background? (*Doubled*, of course, with fifty percent more in residuals!)

Finally, the advertising agencies fought back. Several

adopted a policy that jingle producers could list only one in-house person as a vocalist, either the composer or arranger, and it had to be someone who actually *sang*. Other agencies said: "Use fewer singers and overdub a few more vocal layers to make up the difference in sound. We're paying the fifty percent anyway!" The bean-counters were taking over.

At the same time, rumbles were beginning in other quarters: the professional jingle singers were complaining to their unions about jobs they were losing to jingle house employees who were taking their places on the union contract; and also about having to perform on sessions with people that really didn't sing.

SAG and AFTRA decided to make an all-out effort to eliminate the practice of *padding the vocal contract*. The unions demanded a meeting with the jingle producers to discuss the issue.

I viewed all this from a polite distance. While my company adhered to all the union payment polices, my Peter Kelley contract allowed me to hire the best singers every time; and because I was being paid for the uses of my music and not my voice, vocal residuals were not my concern. I had also learned my lessons from "Breakaway" and Budweiser, and I could not imagine under any circumstances ever giving up all future interests in my music for a one-time fee. Somewhere I had read that, "Progress begins with one word . . . no." I had learned to say "no" to terms that I found unacceptable, and to the standard agency music contract. But no one else in the jingle business ever said "no."

It takes a crisis to bring people together. The industry's income that so heavily relied on vocal residuals was now being seriously challenged by the unions. Calls went out to all the jingle houses in town (myself included, even though everyone knew I was not in the composer-who-sang camp) to attend an intra-industry meeting at one of the big recording studios.

It was the first time I had the opportunity to put faces together with the names I had been hearing through the years: Joey Levine of Crushing Music; David Lucas and Tom McFaul; Susan Hamilton, Bernie Drayton, and Jake Holmes of H.E.A. Music; Ginny Reddington and Tom Dawes; all successful, talented composers and producers who sang on their commercials. Many seemed to know each other. I later learned that some of the big jingle producers would often hire each other as singers when they were in a job competition for a major account, thereby insuring the top cats of a vocal residual no matter whose music won the job.

As each person rose to introduce himself, and guardedly share his ideas about what was wrong with the business, it became clear how differently they all operated from the way I did. The vocal residual was the life-blood of every company: if their ability to be listed on the union contracts was lost, it would be devastating for everyone.

I didn't fit the pattern. When my turn came, I spoke out against the vocal residual, and stated my belief that there was no safety in the unwritten word of an agency producer who promised a jingle house the right to rearrange future versions of their music, and thereby the transparent ability to hire the vocalists. I expressed my belief that a creative fee should not be a one-time kiss-off, and that if everyone sought some form of ongoing payment for the ongoing uses of their compositions—the same as composers of all other kinds of music—and gave up the right to sing in return as a bargaining chip, it would benefit everyone and avoid unnecessary confrontations with the unions. From my point of view, jingle composers should be fighting to retain their creative rights; and to change the unfair terms of the standard agency music contract. We were an infant industry about to come of age, and taking the easy way of jumping on the bandwagon of residuals that had been won by someone else was missing the mark. For the future of our businesses, we needed to carve out our own payment system, and not spend our energy protecting the vocal residual. I said this over and over.

They all thought I was crazy. Abandon the instant gratification of singing in return for being treated like all other songwriters? *Why? We've got a good thing going here; all we have to do is keep it under control.* They wouldn't even discuss the subject. It was like trying to convince someone who was earning a million dollars a year that they were doing something wrong. Susan Hamilton, head of H.E.A. Music Company, stated: "What's good for H.E.A. is good for the jingle industry," parodying the famous "What's good for General Motors is good for America" comment by GM chairman Alfred P. Sloan. *Singing* was good for them. Good enough, anyway.

Everyone did agree, however, that a continuing forum for exchanging views was positive, and the Society of Advertising Producers Arrangers and Composers (SAMPAC), the first-ever jingle industry trade association, was formed.

Shortly thereafter, we all attended a union meeting, supervised by both SAG and AFTRA officials. I joined my new colleagues as they defended their singing policies, hoping my support would help even though I disagreed with their basic business premise. I made the point that the unions did not have the legal authority to dictate to any employer about whom they could hire; that craft unions were not in the business of judging talent; that as long as singers were being paid under union conditions, even though they were not the exact singers that the union might have wanted, no one was breaking any rules. I even went so far as to put the unions on notice that SAMPAC was ready to actively defend any signatory member whose ability to hire whomever they wanted as a vocalist was threatened. Finally, I pointed out that while the contracts were negotiated between the ad agencies and the unions, it was the jingle producers who set and controlled the working conditions in the studios.

Bud Wolfe, AFTRA's Executive Secretary, adamantly took issue with this last point, stating unequivocally that the unions were the only entity that could set working conditions. After the meeting, I pointed out to my colleagues that if management were to take the position that we, the jingle houses, actually set working conditions, it would weaken the union's bargaining position, something that we did not want to do. *Losing the backing of AFTRA and SAG would do more damage to the vocal residual than anything else.* It was to our benefit to completely support the unions.

This crisis was defused. The industry had called the unions' bluff and dodged the bullet. Everyone felt better. For the moment.

SAMPAC tried to schedule monthly meetings, but with the union complaints now on the back burner, the major jingle producers were nowhere to be found. At first, some sent secretaries or assistants in their places; but soon, it was taking a lot of phone-begging and faxing (before e-mail) just to get colleagues to show up at all. Those who did rarely completed whatever tasks they had promised to do at the previous meeting: to put together an industry mailing list; or to draft a set of trade-association by-laws; or to contact an attorney to learn about a specific legal point. The same three or four or five colleagues from smaller jingle houses usually showed up, but without an issue that everyone considered vital, the heavyweights were not interested.

I always felt like somewhat of an outsider, advocating an agenda that was clearly beyond the reach of most. But that was SAMPAC's purpose, I told myself, to openly share experiences and information with the hope that members could improve their ways of doing business. We should be *competitors* on a creative level only: on business matters we were always *col-*

leagues. I had achieved the terms I wanted by saying "no" when I had to; and I reasoned that if everyone would be willing to fight for composer rights, it would make selling my deal that much easier. So I stuck it out, hoping my example would inspire others. I offered my contract form to anyone who asked: many took it; no one used it.

It was soon clear that SAMPAC had been organized to protect the wrong thing: all everyone wanted was to maintain the *singing* status quo. No one was willing to face the risky business issues that could make a difference for the entire industry. "You can't fight City Hall," was the prevailing attitude about the standard agency music contract.

Several interviewees for this book, wistfully recalling the opportunities of the SAMPAC days, told me: "We should have at least tried for something more." My response: "The industry wasn't ready to say 'no.'" Sadly, it still isn't ready. And, unfortunately, "no" would accomplish a lot less today.

To keep SAMPAC breathing, we attempted to identify other sources of ongoing income that might augment or replace vocal residuals.

One issue kept coming up: performance income from the American Society of Composers Authors and Publishers (ASCAP). This was something I had not paid any attention to because I thought it had nothing to do with the advertising agency–jingle composer relationship. Performance royalty, like mechanicals—royalties from the sale of records and CDs—were issues normally thought of only in the record business, the popular songwriting business, not the advertising business. But the more we talked about it, the more we learned that it didn't matter whether music was created for a record or for a commercial: performance royalties were being paid out to composers and publishers through ASCAP all the time; and the money was not coming from the *advertisers*, but from the *radio and television stations!*

SAMPAC began to host industry information seminars, and invite ad agency producers, business managers, and lawyers for a wide-ranging exchange of views. For us, these face-to-face Q&A sessions provided the opportunity to let the advertising community know that we were out there. SAMPAC also hired a PR firm to place stories about industry issues in trade publications. But for the agencies, these meetings were viewed as not much more than a cordial opportunity to tell us as a group the same things they had been telling us individually: you can't change the standard agency music contract.

J. Walter Thompson Advertising (JWT) was then one of the largest ad agencies in the world, a successful old-line company with a do-it-by-the-book reputation. Thompson enjoyed a long history of servicing major clients, and was the classic motion-picture model for the public's perception of the attitudes and mannerisms of the advertising business.

Thompson's business manager, Marion Preston, was a very smart, articulate, unbendable supporter of the standard agency music contract. She served as a trustee on several union pension funds; advocated the agencies' positions in labor negotiations; and ran Thompson's business affairs with an iron fist. To me, she was management personified and as tough in saying "no" to support her business policies as I had become in defending mine.

I had been asked to write for Thompson's clients a few times through the years, but never did because Ms. Preston would never accept my contract form. Only once did I crack that barrier. Tony Amendola—the former creative director at D'Arcy Advertising in St. Louis and the man who selected my music and authorized my deal with Budweiser—had become the president of Schlitz Beer, a J. Walter Thompson client. He wanted me to write music to try and rejuvenate that failing national brand. As usual, Ms. Preston objected to using my contract with its revolutionary terms, but Tony—now "the client"—simply told her to "sign it." When I sent Marion a draft, along with my standard instructions *to print it on JWT letterhead, sign, and return it to us for countersignature,* she was not a happy camper. She called, attempting to change specific language, stating forcefully that Thompson would *never* allow this kind of document. I refused, assuring her I would not work without it. Tony backed me up, and it was a done deal.

Yet with all its rigid, one-sided attitudes towards music suppliers, J. Walter Thompson had become an industry pioneer when it formed a music publishing company to collect performance income from ASCAP. Ms. Preston understood that royalties from ASCAP were being paid by the broadcasters, and JWT had set up a small department to provide all the paperwork that ASCAP required. Thompson's modest performance income was split with the various clients whose commercials used original music; and though they had no real knowledge about the music business, sponsors liked the idea of indirectly getting something back from the broadcasters to whom they were paying all that money to air their commercials. Since ASCAP will not pay royalties to a music *publisher* without also paying a *composer*, the otherwise one-sided Thompson music contract provided the first industry glimmer of ongoing income for the jingle composer, even though it was on a very short leash.

At one SAMPAC seminar about music publishing and "continuance fees" (the industry term for that wished-for, but never-achieved ongoing payment for uses of jingle *compositions,* and not for voices), Ms. Preston indicated that the ad agencies would never agree to another level of residual payments. Singers, actors, and announcers were all getting residuals, and if composers got one, then film directors would want one; then film editors, and the list would be endless. "If you want ongoing income for music," she said, "get it from ASCAP."

In the early days of my career, when I was scoring my porno films, I had joined Broadcast Music, Inc. (BMI) as a composer and publisher, but had switched to ASCAP when I entered the advertising music business because BMI didn't pay anything for jingle performances then, while ASCAP did.

In the grand scheme of composer income sources, Ms. Preston was absolutely right: if we wanted to be treated with the same respect as other songwriters, we should be able to tap the same sources of income as other songwriters.

I agreed to look into the ASCAP matter on behalf of the industry.

I didn't know it then, but I had committed myself to a twenty-year journey that was to eclipse all the other legal battles in my career.

Someone once gave me a little statue of a smug British barrister, wig and all, with the inscription "Sue the Bastards!" on the pedestal. I guess it appealed to my defensively independent self-employed personality. It stood on my desk for many years, until one day, I saw it from a whole new perspective and threw it away.

But I had not yet reached that day. While my colleagues were struggling with how to protect their fragile but lucrative vocal residuals, I began fighting the kind of legal battles I thought all of us should have been fighting.

I discovered that owning a copyright as a music publisher involved much more than just paying a fee, sending a few papers to Washington, and filing away the certificate. Copyright ownership is the essence of the American dream: you create something, and the law gives you certain rights in the uses of that creation, but only as long as you do your part. A copyright is only as valuable as the ability and willingness to defend it; if you don't defend your work against the first misuse, you weaken the defenses against subsequent misuses.

How simple it would be just to write songs and earn money without undertaking all that legal responsibility. The music business is filled with horror stories about songwriters being ripped off by unscrupulous users who took advantage of creative innocence. I tried my best not to be innocent, but I was to learn quickly that there were always smarter business people out there. I respect the T-shirt that says, "Age and Treachery Will Always Overcome Youth and Enthusiasm."

During the interviews for this book, one colleague suggested that if my Budweiser case were heard today, I would surely win. But having witnessed some very skillful shark lawyers exploit the subtle differences between a *contract* and a *license*—trying to gain any advantage for the entity that is paying them—to expect the other side to ever "do the right thing" is a major mistake. The attorney I hired during the Budweiser defense once stated to me that "law cases are not decided on the issues, but by the quality of counsel." I thought about that a lot after losing and paying his bill.

Running my own company was teaching me that advertising agency business managers, and their attorneys and clients, have absolutely nothing to risk when they decide to go out into the field and crush some upstart that dares to roil the waters. The agency employee knows that he will still receive his salary at the end of the week. That kind of paid self-righteousness makes it almost impossible for a small business owner to carry on a successful legal dispute with a big company. And the big guys know it, and that's why they always win.

Legal fees are paid out of the corporate pot, and lawyers will work for which ever side writes the biggest check. Defense attorney Johnny Cochran has said: "The color of justice is green."

There's a classic story about Abraham Lincoln, who as a young country lawyer had argued and won a case in the morning, and that afternoon found himself before the same judge, arguing a case with a similar issue, but this time Lincoln was representing the exact opposite point of view. The judge asked, "Mr. Lincoln, how could you have be so eloquent this morning about one side of this issue and now take the exact opposite position?" Lincoln answered, "Your honor, this morning I was wrong."

Yep, that's the same guy who freed the slaves and saved the Union. I like to think he outgrew his lawyer phase.

I say it a lot: The only safety is in copyright ownership and the protection of a fair contract. I still believe in the law, but after some pretty jarring experiences, I also believe that the system doesn't work.

I was to have a few "warm-up" bouts—my *out-of-town try-outs*—before I got into the ring for the main event against ASCAP.

In 1970, "When You Say Bud" had become an award-winning anthem for Budweiser Beer, and two songwriters in Nashville wrote "When You Say *Love*," an exact imitation of my song. Bob Luman made the first recording. It was played only on country stations, and I never heard it; but when Sonny and Cher did a version, it climbed on to the Billboard Top 100. This was a new kind of problem for me, and as a courtesy to Anheuser Busch I asked if they would like to pursue the matter. They weren't interested, stating that they were in the beer business, not the music business; and because my company owned the music publishing rights to "When You Say Bud," it was my copyright to defend. After a few ignored letters to the publisher of "When You Say *Love*," I hired attorneys and brought suit. In their pre-trial depositions, the two country songwriters made the excuse that they had never heard my hit jingle before because every time a commercial came on radio or TV they changed the station.

Yeah, sure.

A point is reached in every legal action where a settlement is proposed, and then the discussion immediately turns to the cost of continuing the fight versus the amount of any possible greater gain. This is where the individual's commitment is tested. After exploring the investment of time and more money to actually go to court to squeeze out every last drop of victory and vindication, in this matter a settlement made sense. It was not a one-hundred-percent victory, but good enough.

The big lesson was that if I had not retained the publishing rights to my song in my contract with Budweiser and filed for a copyright (as well as for copyrights to all the rearrangements of "When You Say Bud"), these two individuals who had found a way to live in America and avoid all commercials could have walked off with the non-advertising income from my song.

The *Saturday Night Live* TV show often begins with a parody of a current hit commercial; inventive, original, and funny. One week, during the energy crisis in the mid 1970s, they used my Exxon "Energy for a Strong America" song, calling it *"Energy for a Gullible America."* My lawyer and I agreed that they should have sought a sync license to use the music, and also to change the lyric. We wrote a letter to NBC.

They didn't want to fight. We settled for a very nominal amount.

A few months later, *Saturday Night Live* did one of their classic skits, with Gilda Radner, John Belushi, Chevy Chase, and Buck Henry as citizens of the biblical cities of Sodom and Gomorrah. It seems that both of these places had a very bad public image, and the solution put forth by the governing council was to create a new advertising campaign with a new jingle, "I Love Sodom." Again, cute, funny, topical humor. Again, we felt that this unauthorized use of "I Love New York" should generate a sync fee.

This time, NBC rejected our demand letter.

Never load a gun unless you are prepared to use it. We filed an action in federal court. A year or so later, in his summary judgment, Judge Gerard Goettel ruled that *Saturday Night Live's* parody of "I Love New York" was considered a "fair use" under the First Amendment rights of the Constitution. We appealed, and lost again. (I have come to completely agree with the judge's opinion.)

However, this small fair-use decision has become a landmark case in the music business, but for other reasons. In addition to his ruling about First Amendment parody rights, the judge also ruled that four notes of music can be sufficiently original to be protected by copyright law. *Elsmere vs. NBC* is now often quoted in plagiarism cases.

I guess I had read the David and Goliath story a few times too many. As I approached the ASCAP performance-income question on behalf of the jingle industry, I still thought it was possible to prevail against the big guys if you believed in the fairness of the issues and had the determination to slug through the process. I was about to learn that a strong belief in fairness means nothing. (Peter Bart's line is worth repeating: "You don't get what's fair, you get what you negotiate.")

Advertising music was being heard all over the place, and as SAMPAC began to act on Marion Preston's "Get it from ASCAP" suggestion, we naïvely expected that after we had made our case we would be welcomed into ASCAP's big-time songwriter family as fellow "Composers, Authors, and Publishers," just like it says over the doorway.

Yeah, sure.

The first time you discover that you are being screwed by your own family, it's tragic. Especially when you don't see it coming.

But when the screwing is overseen and permitted by the United States government that is supposed to protect your interests, the implications are historic.

It was very important to me that this next section represent the voice of ASCAP today. To accomplish that, I tried to contact executives at ASCAP many times to be interviewed, to update their positions about advertising music, and how they relate to their membership in general. Sadly, they still don't react well to hearing my name at One Lincoln Plaza.

Specifically: I called both the ASCAP Executive Vice President of Membership and ASCAP's CEO *thirteen* times over a two-month period. (With ASCAP you learn to keep records of things like frequency of phone calls and dates). I made clear on each of their voice mails, and to each of their assistants when a live person would answer, that an interview for this book would not be confrontational, that all the battles were long over, and all I wanted was current information. No one ever returned my calls. I describe this frustrating phone-calling process here because it represents one of ASCAP's classic ways of avoiding and delaying any issue raised by a member that might challenge their way of doing business.

I then called an attorney at the United States Department of Justice to include their position about how ASCAP operates today. The Anti-Trust Division has been overseeing ASCAP's activities for more than sixty years. I had visited Washington several times during our "industry protest," and considered myself to be on a cordial business basis with those in charge.

This time, however, before anyone would even talk with me, I had to agree that I would not write anything in this book *for attribution*. "No problem," I said. Again, I made the non-confrontational speech; that "the war was long over." A few weeks later, someone called to schedule a phone call for a few weeks later (in the dictionary under "slow," there is a picture of the US Justice Department), and when that day finally arrived, there was also a member of the Justice Department Public Relations Division on the line monitoring the conversation. (Sounds like the Cuban Missile Crisis, doesn't it? Did you know that the Department of Justice has a PR division? I didn't. I wonder if they recorded the call.) We talked in general terms about where things are today, and of course I will honor my agreement and not attribute anything of substance to any specific individual.

Everyone at ASCAP and at the anti-trust division knows me very well. I led the twenty-year industry fight for a higher jingle payment rate.

If you have gained any sense of who I am from reading this book so far, you will know that I did not take any of this lightly.

The story begins long before I got involved, with some necessary background:

ASCAP was founded in the early 1900s by Irving Berlin and the other top popular songwriters of that era to collect income when their songs were used in live public performances—in theatres, saloons, outdoor concerts, etc. Backed up by the new 1909 copyright law that had just been passed by Congress to protect *intellectual property rights*, the concept was wonderfully simple: each venue would be charged a fee and required to provide a list of the songs they used to ASCAP, which would then divide the income between those composers and music publishers whose songs were played. This was during the era of silent movies, long before "talkies," or any of the other types of music usage that grew naturally out of advancing technology. *Popular songs* were what people wanted, and popular songs were what ASCAP licensed. In idealistic terms, there was much to be admired: ASCAP would be a clearing house for songwriters and music publishers who were prepared to stand together to defend their rights and achieve a common objective, something that the jingle composers of later generations were unwilling to do.

When radio was invented (and later television), ASCAP applied the same concept, issuing what was called a *blanket license* to the stations (the broadcasters) which could pick and choose from any of the music in the ASCAP catalog, report the titles of the songs back to ASCAP, and the income, after operating expenses, would be divided among those whose music was played. Soon, ASCAP represented literally all of the top songwriters in America.

In 1940, the radio stations complained to the Federal Government that they were being charged outrageously high license fees by ASCAP and since ASCAP was the only Performing Rights Organization in existence, that it was a monopoly. The Justice Department agreed, and sued ASCAP under anti-trust laws.

In settlement of the suit (which took *twenty years* to resolve, an indication of how ASCAP management was even then successfully able to drag its legal feet), ASCAP's Board of Directors, comprised entirely of popular-song and *standards* composers and publishers, pulled off one of the slickest jobs ever of duping the Federal government. Under the loud guise of representing the interests of *all types* of music, ASCAP convinced the Justice Department to permit a "category" system for royalty distributions, and they gave *popular songs* the highest payment rate (100% of a credit), while all other categories were assigned much lower percentages: TV themes, 33%; TV background scores, 16%; and advertising music, 1% of a credit. The actual dollar-value of each *credit* would be based on the income ASCAP received from the stations, and adjusted periodically using mystical mathematics that have never been divulged to the membership,

This confusing "weighting formula" has been one of ASCAP's strongest tools in avoiding accurate payment to those whose music is actually heard. No matter how much time people take to study it—lawyers, statisticians, laymen, *anyone*—no one understands it.

The Justice Department, ever naïve to the wily ways of the

music business, accepted ASCAP's rationale that popular songs were entitled to be paid more than all other types of music because, at that time, in 1960, radio broadcasting was mainly Top 40 music programming; and network television was filled with popular-song driven variety shows such as *The Perry Como Show*, *The Patti Page Show*, *The Ed Sullivan Show*, and *Your Hit Parade*.

But at the same time as it was telling the Justice Department that it was appropriate to distribute income based on separate musical *categories*, ASCAP was insisting on charging the broadcasters under a one-fee concept—the blanket license. ASCAP would not permit the stations to pay only for the specific music they wanted to broadcast, but made them pay for the right to use *all* the music in the ASCAP repertory. That meant ASCAP's income—based upon a negotiated percentage of the stations revenue—would not be earned from the uses of any specific categories of music, but that royalty distributions to members would be made *only* under a category system; and the division of the pie left exclusively up to the ASCAP Board of Directors, again, all of whom were *popular* song composers and publishers. Forcing the stations to pay for all music effectively took the determination of the *value* of each category of music out of the marketplace, and left the determination of how much each category was worth exclusively to ASCAP's Board of Directors.

Of course, not knowing anything about the music business, the government said, "Yes."

ASCAP's view of advertising music, then worth only one percent of a payment credit for a custom-made jingle, changed dramatically when one of their popular songs was licensed for a commercial. That use would earn fifty percent of a credit (fifty times more!) for exactly the same sixty or thirty seconds of air time!

Twice through the years, the broadcasters tried to eliminate the blanket license, wanting to only pay for the music they actually used. But ASCAP prevailed in both the "CBS Case" and the "Buffalo Broadcasting Case" by convincing the courts that all the paperwork required for the stations to obtain individual licenses each time they wanted to use a song would be impossible, and therefore a hardship for all songwriters. The blanket license system survived, and as a critical afterthought, so did the biased category system for royalty distributions.

The best hoodwink was yet to come: in addition to permitting ASCAP's Board to award the old-time standards composers and publishing interests (themselves) extra payments for the longevity of their works, ASCAP was also allowed to establish a weighted *voting* process. Those composers and publishers whose songs had been played the most through the years now received more votes in each ASCAP Board of Director election. Not temporary one-time votes; but when a song had attained a certain number of airplays, the extra vote that was awarded became *permanent*. And cumulative! Board members were building a savings bank of votes with which to self-perpetuate themselves in office and maintain unchallenged control of the distribution system!

And the Justice Department said, "Yes."

At a 1957 ASCAP membership meeting, Oscar Hammerstein II, one of ASCAP's greatest lyricists, and also one of the strongest voices to keep the non-popular songwriters in their places, summed up his views about the weighted voting system:

> "I think there is one basic thing that we ought to face, and that is that ASCAP is not, and does not pretend to be, a democracy. ASCAP is a group of property owners. Let us get that into our head. This is not the United States; it is more like United States Steel. Do not think that the people who own a whole lot of property in this, and many copyrights, are going to take one vote, the same vote as

the man who owns one copyright. Don't think that, and don't waste our time, and don't waste yours: that is not going to happen; for the day it does happen ASCAP is going to be broken up and the devil take the hindmost . . . and you know who the hindmost are going to be: the people with the good copyrights."

Mr. Hammerstein's opinion that the category of popular songs, particularly standards, are the "good" ASCAP copyrights, and all other categories are not, still rules at ASCAP today.

Now that ASCAP management had obtained the keys to the vault, they began to slowly and methodically solidify their control over the entire system.

In order to convince the Justice Department that they were going to treat the rank and file membership honestly, the following sentence was inserted into what is called "The 1960 Amended Final Judgment":

"Defendant ASCAP is hereby ordered and directed to distribute to its members the monies received by licensing rights of public performance on a basis which gives primary consideration to the performances of compositions of the members as indicated by objective surveys of performances (excluding those licensed by the member directly) periodically made by or for ASCAP."

It is ASCAP management's vehement interpretation of this order that the "objective surveys of performances" are merely to *identify* which songs are played—*Name That Tune*—and then continue to distribute income based on the weighted *category* system: and that they are not required to adjust the category payment percentages based on changing musical tastes in the marketplace.

Also, in that famous paragraph, ASCAP members are *excluded* from presenting their own objective surveys of performances, thereby rendering ASCAP management completely and legally insulated against anyone other than the Board of Directors being able to present an acceptable survey.

ASCAP was being run by very smart people. To maintain the appearance of even-handedness, ASCAP created the post of "Special Distribution Advisor." These would be filled by two "outside" attorneys to whom ASCAP could refer any member questions about how the system worked. (The Special Advisors would function much like the Commissioner of Baseball. I remember in my youth, when there was a dispute between a player and his team, the public would always anxiously await the ruling of the Commissioner. The public was as naïve as the Justice Department: no one wanted to realize that the Commissioner of Baseball was hired and paid by the team owners! Did anyone seriously expect that he would ever rule *against* management? The only Commissioner of Baseball in my memory who ever ruled for a player against the owners was Fay Vincent. He received an immediate vote of "no confidence" and *resigned* the next day.)

Of course, the Justice Department said "yes" to everything.

All these rules and formulae were set down in what is called a "Consent Decree," which was approved by the federal court.

The government was now officially in the music business.

That was the ASCAP world SAMPAC entered seeking the financial respect as songwriters that the advertising industry had never given us.

In 1979, colleagues began to question why advertising music, arguably the most often-heard category of music in America, was still only paid 1% of an ASCAP credit, the same rate that had been in effect since the Amended Judgment of 1960. A meeting was set up at ASCAP to discuss our concerns.

ASCAP is always willing to meet with complaining members. Meetings take time to organize, time to attend, more time to consider the conversations afterwards, and before anyone knows it, months and months have passed with nothing changed. When you are a jingle composer worried about winning a job competition or keeping your ability to be listed on the union vocal contract, having a meeting at ASCAP is a powerful tool of diversion—for ASCAP.

ASCAP's Chairman of the Board, Stanley Adams, was courteous; the few other Board members who attended the meeting smiled a lot; and ASCAP General Counsel, Bernard Korman, articulated all the reasons why the current distribution system was being fair to all members. "There is only one pie," Mr. Korman said, "and everyone has to have an equitable piece of it."

After this polite, informal, but firm "no," SAMPAC retained a lawyer, who wrote a long flowing letter to ASCAP, detailing why jingle music should earn more than 1% of a credit. The legal fee bill for this letter was an astounding $14,000.

Mr. Korman responded with his own long flowing letter, explaining that, after examining some of the contracts that colleagues had submitted to ASCAP to support their claim for higher payment, one of the main reasons ASCAP could not pay more for advertising music was that jingle composers *did not own the right to public performances of their works* that ASCAP needed in order to license music to the stations—they had *signed them away to the agencies in the standard agency music contract!*

However, ASCAP said it would look into the matter.

We believed that ASCAP had included the category of jingles in its payment scheme as window dressing, merely to show the world that their blanket license represented all types of music. Only J. Walter Thompson's music company and a very few others, including my own, were regularly registering advertising works with ASCAP to qualify for performance income.

ASCAP's very wise management then took the long view: when you grant someone a raise, it becomes a great tool of defense against another raise. One day, we received word that the Board of Directors had magnanimously increased the jingle rate from the lowly 1% of a credit to the exalted 3% of a credit. A 300% increase! Wow! SAMPAC members thought this increase was ludicrously insufficient, certainly not enough incentive to make jingle composers begin to fight for their rights with the agencies and change the standard agency music contract.

Round one to ASCAP.

In 1980, when "I Love New York" was proclaimed the official song of New York State, ASCAP seized the opportunity to have some dialogue. ASCAP's director of publicity, Karen Sherry, invited me to ASCAP's offices where pictures were taken for ASCAP's magazine. General Counsel Bernard Korman invited me to lunch to describe again how fair the system was, and to again state that ASCAP had only one income pie to divide, and that when one category got more, naturally another had to take less. When I questioned the basic fairness of the category system, Mr. Korman suggested that perhaps the jingle community should form its own performance rights society and license works directly to the broadcasters. Of course, he said, ASCAP would still keep jingles in its blanket license, but maybe we would be better off elsewhere. (This "if you don't like it, you can leave" attitude would later become a strong ASCAP device to maintain its control over the Justice Department and the federal courts.) Then, ASCAP Board member and pop-song lyricist Sammy Cahn called—we knew each other casually as fellow members of the Friars Club— and at dinner one night Sammy expressed his belief that if

ASCAP were ever to be broken up, it would not come from some outside source, such as the broadcasters, but from within the ASCAP membership. I told Mr. Cahn that I was honored to be part of ASCAP and to have my music counted along side of his; and that I owned my copyrights the same as he did and that I had no desire to fight. *Wasn't ASCAP formed to distribute income to those whose music was played? The marketplace had changed. Advertising music was everywhere.* When I described vocal residuals, Mr. Cahn had no idea what I was talking about.

There is something in a songwriter's psyche that does not respond well to rejection, even though it is coated with candy. Some shrug, swallow their pride, and walk away. I just couldn't walk away. I was a member of an organization that wasn't giving my music a fair shake. I had once been told by the local country club not to apply for membership because I was Jewish. Since then, each winter, I cross-country ski on their golf course, and pee on their greens. I've become quite adept at making a Star of David in the snow. The 3% jingle rate was the same kind of discrimination, and it pushed all the same buttons.

I decided to seek election as Chairman of SAMPAC, hoping that colleagues would support a further effort to change the ASCAP distribution system. Members agreed and, over time, we paid off our $14,000 legal fee obligation. I found new lawyers who were willing to work on an expenses-only contingency basis, agreeing to accept one third of any increase they could win.

In order to prove that advertising music was entitled to a much higher percentage rate, we commissioned an air study of our own (costing $40,000), even though such studies were prohibited by ASCAP's rules. The Bruskin Report showed that advertising music represented 41% of all music heard on television, and 12% of all music heard on radio. From our point of view, the raise from 1% to 3% was merely a band aid put out by ASCAP to shut us up. (The increase, of course, had been rubberstamped by the Department of Justice and the federal court, which each had the right of approval over all rate changes as required in the Consent Decree.)

In hindsight, our effort to change the distribution system was to become the most serious threat ASCAP management had faced since the anti-trust suit brought by the government in 1940. And they knew it. And we didn't. We just wanted a realistic jingle rate as incentive for composers to retain their rights, either in their own publishing companies or through the many newly formed advertising agency music publishing companies.

If ASCAP had thrown us a reasonable bone by raising the jingle rate to, say, 10% or 15% of a credit, all of what followed would never have happened. But paying jingles more would be taking money out of Board members' own pockets. I used to wonder why the TV theme/film-scoring community never complained about being second-class citizens to the popular song when their music was dominating TV broadcasting. Then I learned that scoring-creative fees plus performance income—even at a less-than-desirable category rate—was enough to keep everybody happy. Any member complaints were usually about why the composer had not been paid for a specific use, something ASCAP could easily quell with a back-payment to make the complainer go away.

No formal *category* class had ever challenged the distribution system. We didn't know it then but ASCAP could *never* allow any group effort to succeed, under any circumstances. Their popular-song superiority was rooted in the single-mindedness of ASCAP's founding fathers, when there were no other categories of music. That's the way they wanted it now. This was life and death for them, the manifestation of Sammy Cahn's challenge from within. We had become an organized threat, not to the 3% jingle rate, but to the 100% popular-song rate and to the way ASCAP had done business for more than seventy years.

How simple it all seemed: we would hire lawyers, let them fight the good fight, and walk away satisfied. No composer wants to devote huge hunks of his life to combat.

It didn't take long to learn that ASCAP's well-oiled machine was prepared to spend whatever funds and time necessary to defeat us.

First, our attorneys were pointedly reminded by Mr. Korman that the ASCAP membership agreement prohibits a composer/publisher from suing ASCAP. Instead, all grievances must be submitted to an *internal* Board of Review, which is elected by the ASCAP membership. (This is an appropriate time to recall the weighted *voting* process, which gave extra votes to those *popular-song* and *standards* composers so they could control the election system.) Then, if the member is not satisfied with the decision of the Board of Review, the rules state that the composer may apply for a further hearing before an impartial Arbitration Committee.

It still sounded doable. We filed the necessary papers.

I was the only member of the jingle community who had retained all the rights necessary to license performances through ASCAP, and colleagues in SAMPAC agreed that the industry protest would be brought in my own name—and not as group effort or class action—thereby eliminating one of ASCAP's strongest arguments against us.

It took two years to complete three separate hearings before the Board of Review, a body made up completely of popular songwriters and one classical music composer. In the legal discovery process prior to the hearings, we learned that ASCAP's rules of protest prohibited a member from seeing documents about how distribution rates are determined; nor can the protestor subpoena or question witnesses about how rates are determined. When we presented our air-study, ASCAP immediately disqualified it because it was not allowed in the Consent Decree. Attorney Bernard Korman testified that "ASCAP thought we were paid enough." Mr. Korman made much of the issue that jingle composers received residuals when their works were broadcast, even though it was untrue. We made the point that the residuals were earned as union *singers*, not as *composers*.

It didn't matter.

In twenty-six pages of high legalese, written by ASCAP management, the Board of Review ruled against our protest. (One of ASCAP's in-house lawyers also held the title of "Counsel to the Board of Review" and was the author of the document.)

We immediately filed for the impartial arbitration allowed at the end of an unsuccessful Board of Review decision. It took another year to finally schedule the hearing, and in their first motion of the day ASCAP advised the Arbitrators that, again under ASCAP rules, they could not hear any new evidence (a trial de novo), but could only base their considerations on the evidence that had been presented at the Board of Review hearings, *where we were not allowed to see documents or question witnesses!*

The Arbitrators had no choice, and ruled against us.

We then appealed to William Conner, the federal judge who had been in charge of the ASCAP Consent Decree for the previous twenty-five years, complaining that without having the ability to question witnesses and examine evidence we had been denied the due process of a fair trial. The judge agreed, sending the matter back to the Arbitrators, giving them a limited right to hear evidence of how the increase from 1% to 3% came about.

ASCAP was furious.

Now, each time I saw Sammy Cahn at the Friars Club, he

would glance at me with one of those I-must-have-stepped-in-something looks, and walk right by.

While all this was going on, SAMPAC began an all-out effort to educate the advertising agencies about ASCAP, holding seminars to demonstrate that performance income would not cost their clients a cent because all royalties were paid by the stations who broadcast the music, and not by the advertisers. Slowly, the agencies woke up, and some formed their own music publishing companies, to divide the "free" income from broadcast performances with their clients. Others made deals with independent music publishers or payroll services that could process the paperwork to ASCAP on their behalves. Suddenly, agencies were willing to provide the "secret" air-schedules that ASCAP demanded to verify performances (a demand they did not place on any other categories of music usage), and ASCAP had to distribute greater sums of money—even at the 3% rate—for advertising works.

We asked the ad agencies to help finance our effort, but "controversy" is a word never heard on Madison Avenue. *Join a legal action against ASCAP?* The agencies would be delighted if someone else achieved a raise for them, but not one was interested in either the time or investment to participate. And each agency had a lawyer with an opinion that had to be considered. Marion Preston's words "Get it from ASCAP" should have continued, "On your own!"

The paperwork was plodding along—thirty days to file a motion with the court; thirty days for ASCAP to respond to the motion; thirty days for us to respond to the response; and on and on with extensions for holidays, and then debating which officers of ASCAP should be allowed to testify before the Arbitrators. I was having a hard time trying to raise funds from SAMPAC members, who by now, without any quick concrete result, had lost interest in this matter, and were busy caring about other things in their lives. Another year passed.

Finally, all sides gathered again as the arbitration panel met to hear Leon Brettler, a member of the ASCAP Distribution Committee, describe the intricate procedure they had followed when they raised the jingle rate from 1% to 3%. This was the dialogue in the committee meeting: "Let's give 'em 5% . . . no, let's give 'em nothing . . . OK, let's split the difference and make the jingle rate 3% . . . and let's get our statistician to come up with a formula to justify the change." So much for ASCAP's "objective" air surveys.

This time, the Arbitrators ruled in our favor, declaring that the increase from 1% to 3% was "arbitrary." It was the first time a member protest had ever beaten ASCAP's system.

ASCAP was shocked. *Shocked!*

This effectively put the jingle rate back to 1%, the rate that was in effect during all the years before our industry's complaining had begun. We naïvely hoped that ASCAP would now realize how wrong they had been, and finally conduct the objective survey called for in the Consent Decree, with more honest and realistic results.

We had yet to fully comprehend what was at stake for the Board if they lost. Someone had thought this all out beforehand. While our lawyers were proudly patting each other on the back, congratulating themselves on the arbitration victory, unknown to us, as soon as they learned of the Arbitrators' negative decision, ASCAP immediately notified the Justice Department that they were reinstating the 3% jingle rate, claiming that a reduction back to 1% would have been an unfair hardship to their members. This magnanimous gesture looked great on paper. The Justice Department, who never says "no" to ASCAP, of course, agreed.

Suddenly, ASCAP's General Counsel Bernard Korman was fired. Board members walked into his office one afternoon, and after forty years of service, he was gone in an hour. No gold watch, nothing. We learned from our attorneys that

ASCAP was tired of fighting with its members all the time, something that the combative Mr. Korman was particularly adept at doing. ASCAP also switched its outside law firm from Paul, Weiss, Rifkind, Wharton and Garrison to White and Case, another big change.

We took this as a glimmer of hope. Maybe there was new thinking that would see things in a more conciliatory way. We appealed to Judge Conner that reinstating the 3% rate was not in the spirit of our arbitration victory. In their response papers, ASCAP told the judge that they had adjusted some internal distribution mechanisms in the jingle formula and had just actually raised the rate, this time by 16%, in theory now making the jingle rate 3.48%. "Mr. Karmen won a 16% increase!" ASCAP said loudly. So much for conciliation.

When a labor union receives a 16% boost in wages, it's considered substantial. But the raise from 3% to 3.48% of a credit was a sham, especially when a popular song still received 100% of a credit.

We went back to Judge Conner again, this time asking him to order ASCAP to perform the objective survey called for in the Consent Decree; or to order the Arbitrators to raise the rate; or order the Arbitrators to order ASCAP to perform an objective air study; or to do something, *anything*, to stop the blatant disregard of the requirements of the Consent Decree.

ASCAP's new lawyers changed strategy: instead of continuing to argue about category rates and air surveys, they now focused on the single issue of whether a member should even have the right to challenge the judgment and experience of ASCAP's duly elected Board of Directors, arguing that an ad hoc arbitration panel should not have the power to interfere in a music distribution system that was being run by the caring, concerned, and professional ASCAP Board.

Judge Conner then delivered the coup de grâce to our protest, saying first that in accordance with the Consent

Decree, the Court's jurisdiction and the Justice Department's only sphere of influence was in ASCAP's relations with the broadcasters, and not with ASCAP's membership. Then he ruled that *only* the Board of Directors and not an ad hoc panel of Arbitrators should have the power to set distribution rates.

The results were announced prominently in the *New York Times*, on radio and TV, and in all the trade papers.

One last time, we went back to Judge Conner, saying that if the rate was really raised by 16% as ASCAP had clearly told the court, at the very least, after fifteen years, we were entitled to a 16% retroactive payment increase back to the beginning of our protest, back to 1981, as is called for under ASCAP's rules. This would have given me the opportunity to pay something to the attorneys whom I had begged to work on a contingency basis through all those years of effort.

Yet again the Judge ruled for ASCAP, saying that, even though I had "won" a 16% increase, ASCAP rules state that *because the increase was not directly awarded by the arbitration panel, the retroactive rule did not apply*. Of course, this was *after* the same judge had ruled that Arbitrators did not have the power to raise rates. Maybe he thought that everyone had forgotten about his first ruling. There is a line of dialogue in the movie *The Terminator* that clearly describes how ASCAP operates: "It can't be reasoned with, it can't be bargained with, it can't be stopped."

By the way, Judge Conner did say that if I was not happy with his decision about retroactive payment, of course, I could go back to the Board of Review, and begin again.

Oh, yeah, sure.

Our protest had taken fifteen years, from 1981 to 1996. The effort proved only one thing: that a member has no power to influence a distribution rate. The kangaroo-court Board of Review/Arbitration Protest process is a meaningless waste of time. ASCAP management is invulnerable to member action because the Court and Justice Department turn a blind eye: membership issues are not anti-trust issues.

To further keep control of the system, ASCAP announced to the membership that they were opening a full-time lobbying office in Washington, to finance and maintain an ongoing influence in any Congressional discussions about music use, including the all-important extensions of the copyright law, which clearly benefit the *standards* publisher members of ASCAP's Board of Directors.

I wrote to everyone on my old contributor list telling them what had happened. We had won the only battle we were permitted to fight under ASCAP's restrictive rules, but we had lost the war. It was over. Our eternal spring of hope had run dry. SAMPAC had long since dissolved for lack of interest, or an issue to rally around. No one cared about ASCAP jingle performances any more. The new generation of music houses had no idea what the fight was all about anyway.

We didn't fail for lack of trying, but because our industry was unwilling to stand up for the same rights that all other composers automatically take for granted. The individual self-serving interests powered by the vocal residual overwhelmed any real hope for a group effort. I like to think that if we were all in it together the outcome might have been different.

Sometime during the years of our ASCAP protest, BMI began to pay for jingle performances. I will not pretend to understand BMI's system; I purposely chose not to follow it. One heartbreak per career was enough. I do know, however, that BMI will pay for a jingle performance only if the commercial contains fifteen consecutive seconds of music heard in the clear. In the world of 30-second spots, that restriction is as effective as the 3% jingle rate at ASCAP.

I was still not yet ready to let this go. One day, I wrote to Judge Conner, asking him to describe what sort of "due process" is available if a member wants to challenge a distribution rate. (As usual, copies of all correspondence were sent to ASCAP and the Justice Department.) The judge passed the buck to the Honorable Harold R. Tyler, one of ASCAP's Special Distribution Advisors, who coincidently happened to be the ASCAP Judge before William Conner. We had four or five letters back and forth, within which Mr. Tyler pleasantly lauded the fairness of the current distribution system while restating all the rulings that had been made by Judge Conner during my protest. Neither jurist ever directly answered the question. Finally, in a moment which must have caused him great pain and sorrow, Judge Tyler wrote that there was a new Consent Decree under consideration and that the position of Special Distribution Advisor would probably be eliminated. (I guess he was going to miss all the perks that came with the job.)

There was a coda in the dirge before the last nail was neatly inserted in our quest-for-respect-and-continuance-fee coffin.

In 1998, I was invited to Washington by the Justice Department. The anti-trust division was holding informal meetings with individual broadcasters, songwriters, publishers, anyone in the music business who was interested in contributing information that might guide the development of a more up-to-date ASCAP Consent Decree. It seemed that all the complaining and legal activity we had endured through the years had not fallen on completely deaf ears. Even the government knew that it was time for a change. The ever-naïve-songwriter part of me perked up once more. It was too late to help the colleagues with whom I had begun the fight all those years ago, but maybe it was a last chance to perhaps make a difference for future generations of composers who might work in advertising.

These were the four points I made:

1) In the forty years since the 1960 Consent Decree, the music business has changed dramatically. Network television is filled with sit-coms, game shows, news magazines, soap operas, and movies-of-the-week, where the only music heard is program themes, background scores, and advertising music, not popular songs. Local television is filled with news shows and syndicated reruns. On radio, where popular music was once king, all-talk formats are now the rage, using only advertising music. When popular songs are broadcast—on music radio stations, the late night TV shows, the occasional seasonal special, or MTV and VH1—they are the Grammy Award songs being written today, and not the old-time *standards*, which continue to earn a premium even though they are not broadcast with anywhere near the frequency to deserve extra credits. Further, through the years, though ASCAP has tinkered with the distribution rates for some of the lower categories, responding to the squeaky-wheel of the moment, the 100% popular song rate has never been changed or questioned.

2) The Consent Decree should be terminated, and the government should get out of the music business. ASCAP is no longer a monopoly, today licensing only 50% of the music broadcast. BMI and SESAC (another performing rights society) control the rest. The broadcasters and ASCAP are perfectly capable of negotiating license fees directly with each other, and having their differences worked out in the courts or in arbitration, as in other healthy businesses. Without the unnecessary hindrance of governmental oversight, the music that brings in the income today could be counted equally with the greats of yesteryear instead of contributing to their endless, undeserved pensions.

3) The ASCAP multi-vote election system should be changed to more realistically represent the interests of those whose music is being played today, not those of the ancient past.

4) The entire category-based distribution system should be scrapped, and replaced with one where a composer's income is determined according to the actual air time his music is broadcast, regardless of biased category. This system, called "durational music," is how the entire world pays for the broadcast uses of music—with the singular exception of the United States.

In 2001, twenty years after we had begun our fight, and with great fanfare, ASCAP announced a new Consent Decree.

For me, it all proved to be nothing more than the same exercise on a different day.

The distribution system remained unchanged.

The election process remained unchanged.

The member protest process remained unchanged.

The only difference was that a member could terminate his membership agreement with more ease than before. That's all our government could come up after forty years: if the member wasn't happy, he could pack up his songs and take a hike.

And, yes, quite sadly, the position of Special Distribution Advisor was eliminated. But, don't worry, boys and girls: two months later ASCAP proudly announced that their two former "advisors" had happily agreed to continue their same efforts on ASCAP's behalf, now under the title of "ombudsman." Hurray! *Long live the Commissioner of Baseball!*

Later that year, even though I was now out of the loop, I was asked by one of the new ad music suppliers to support the election of a library-music owner to the ASCAP Board of Directors. I was told that if this candidate—"our" candidate—

could crack into the exclusive pop-song club, it might start the process of making a difference; and that he would be our "strong voice of protest." I wrote and called others and signed petitions, and with the support of everyone in the business, and much to the chagrin of ASCAP management, our candidate was elected. Maybe he would now begin to accomplish what we were unable to do through twenty long years of legal conflict.

But instead of saying "no" to everything that ASCAP wanted, as he had promised, and rattling their cages, as he promised, and making his presence felt even though he was one single vote against the other twenty-three popular-song members that controlled the Board, our elected "strong voice of protest" wimped out.

When it came time for the ASCAP Board to formally ratify the "new" Consent Decree, he voted with the Board, giving ASCAP management the right to brag to the world that the Board approval had been *unanimous!* When I angrily chastised him for abandoning the people who had elected him to office, our new Director said that he saw no purpose in antagonizing anyone; nor did he see a difference between *unanimous* approval by the Board and *overwhelming* approval by the Board.

I did.

I saw a huge difference between 24–0 and 23–1.

We had elected Benedict Arnold.

Two years later when Mr. Arnold was up for reelection, there was no doubt that he would win again: all the other members of the Board with all their extra votes would surely want him to continue to serve: his presence on the Board legitimized their activities.

Of course, he was reelected, and will probably continue to be so.

Some days the dragon wins. The ASCAP dragon had

enjoyed a twenty-year meal.

When I interviewed my "not-for-attribution" source at the Justice Department for this book, he admitted to me that the government had washed its hands of ASCAP because no one really understands how ASCAP works anyway, and the anti-trust division was on to other issues, like fighting with Microsoft.

As an unfortunate side effect of my legal jingle journey, ASCAP now quotes the rules it established under the "Karmen Protest" to squelch any other member complaints.

The changes that were about to occur in the advertising music business would not be a random accident or simply an evolution of consumer tastes. ASCAP's successful effort to keep jingles in their low place had been carefully orchestrated and was directly related to the rising use of popular songs in commercials. Jingles had been a mere annoyance to ASCAP for years, but when we started to make noise the big music publishers realized how much money they could be making— not by encouraging the creation of jingles and giving us some standing in the musical community, as we had hoped—but by making their popular songs more attractive and available for use in advertising. Ironically, we actually brought to their attention the lucrative field they had ignored. The romance between the jingle house and the agencies was ending, and being replaced by a new romance between music publishers and agencies.

As costs for vocal residuals got out of hand, it became financially prudent for sponsors to look elsewhere for their music. The popular-song publishers that have forever controlled the ASCAP Board of Directors were joining forces with the few major record companies, and these giants were hungry, ready, and waiting.

Chapter 8

The Unraveling

The ducks were still happily flapping around in the pond, squawking and squabbling among themselves, completely unaware of the hunter who was sitting comfortably in his blind, watching, sipping his martini, scheming and dreaming of the delicious dinners that lay ahead.

It's too easy to blame technology for the sea changes that have happen to mankind since the invention of the wheel, but the arrival of the electronic synthesizer in the early 1980s surely changed the music business forever. One musician, using a *controller keyboard* that looked like a piano, was able to produce the synthesized sounds of every instrument in the orchestra, as well as create a whole new dictionary of never-before-heard *digital* sounds. The analog multi-track tape machine was fading into oblivion; now all music, old or new, could be converted into a digital format and easily stored on the hard drive of a computer, instantly available and editable with the click of a mouse.

At first, jingle producers stuck their toes gently into the new hi-tech water. Synthesizer players, mostly young musicians who understood the new language of sequencing programs, began showing up at the end of sessions, bringing with them portable racks of the latest computers, samplers, and cutting-edge digital equipment to overdub little dashes of electronic salt-and-pepper to the otherwise live-musician performances. Agency clients were fascinated with all the new sounds that could be created by one person at the touch of a button.

The old-time studio musicians hated it.

Then with the speed of a grace note, every jingle supplier had set up their own in-house *MIDI-studio* and, with the good old gang still doing all the singing, could now crank out demos without having to worry about recording time charges or the hourly AF of M fee. And this drummer never got tired or needed a coffee break!

The appeal of the one-man synth band awoke a brand-new agency budget argument: "Can the public tell the difference between a live drummer and a drum machine? Between a real brass section and one that had been sampled? There's going to be an announcer over it anyway; why spend all that money on live musicians?" Agencies began to expect their demos to be air-quality. One agency music director stated: "The technology was there, everyone had it, and there was no excuse for less." Two or three days' turnaround time became the norm, as composers tried to beat their competition to the starting gate and position themselves first in the agency-recall memory bank.

Soon, anyone with a keyboard and a computer was becoming a music supplier, working in a home/office studio, creating even more competition for the available jobs. Formal musical training was unnecessary. All the composer had to do was get it right once—or *almost* right—and a computer could do the rest: correct wrong notes, speed up tempos, *quantize* the rhythm so the electronic drummer sounded like Ringo Starr or

Charlie Watts. String-section runs could be built one note at a time, with one finger. Shrek now had the ability to arrange like Gordon Jenkins. If needed, a computer program could even print out the music, but for most composers that became redundant as the copyright office in Washington took notice of the new world of digital songwriters and began accepting audio cassettes and CDs of compositions for copyright registration without a written leadsheet.

The AF of M could do nothing about this Frankenstein replacement for live musicians. Synth music and its instant convenience were literally sounding the death-knell of the studio-musician era. Quincy Jones, the world-class record producer and Hollywood arranger, is reputed to have joked before beginning a session with a hundred-piece orchestra: "Looks like we put two synth players out of work."

Jingle producers, on the other hand, had found a new source of revenue with which to torment their agency employers. Instead of listing the names of the *live* string players and *live* horn players and *live* WHATEVER players on the AF of M jingle contract, now they began listing their *own* names as synthesizer players, as many times as traffic would allow. After all, they said, using the tried-and-true argument, even though only one person was creating the track, it was using technology that had replaced many, and the individual who was skilled enough to understand and operate this newfangled equipment ought to be paid accordingly. Jingle producers began submitting AF of M contracts listing Joe Smith—drums; Joe Smith—bass; Joe Smith—violins; Joe Smith—keyboards; Joe Smith—French horns; Joe Smith—trombones; Joe Smith—trumpets. Some synth/composers were pushy enough to list Joe Smith—first violins; Joe Smith—second violins; Joe Smith—violas; Joe Smith—celli, breaking the string section into its normal parts. For a while, Joe Smith was doing really well, especially in residuals, which were earned for each sep-

141

arate listing on the contract. One jingle house listed Joe Smith *twenty-seven* times, and got away with it.

Once.

This time the agencies were ready. They had learned their lessons from the composer/singers who had overdubbed eight-times to earn eight-times vocal residuals, and they began restricting the number of times Joe Smith could appear on the AF of M contract. Some agencies permitted the same name three times; some five times; some only once—at double scale; whatever minimal number they could pressure the jingle house into accepting. It was never a negotiation: you took the agencies' terms or you didn't get the job. And it didn't matter how many actual hours it took to complete the construction of a digital music track; the synth player–composer was still allowed only *one* hour of scale payment on the contract.

Suppliers wanted to be compensated for their investment in all this new high-tech gadgetry. The studio costs to record a *live* orchestra, by comparison, now appeared cheap as music houses tried to bill their clients for the forty or fifty hours of time it was taking to finish a digital job. Again, the agencies fought back, and were soon dictating to the jingle houses *their* estimate of how long it should take to complete an assignment. Most ad agency music directors had started out as either assistants in recording studios or as employees of jingle houses and knew how the business worked from the inside. *We have twelve hours of studio time in our budget. Can you do the job?*

The jingle houses never said, "No."

By the mid 1990s, digital music had become indistinguishable from the real thing; in fact, to the public and to the professional as well, electronic sounds *were* the real thing. Drum-machine patterns and hard-rock guitar licks were being used as stand-alone background tracks for commercials, with no discernable melody or consumer memorability. Occasionally, a real guitar player might be added to an electronic rhythm section to give it a *live* feel, but most often that was deemed unnecessary, especially during the demo stage. Certainly, there were still *live*-orchestra sessions, but the bread-and-butter jobs, the tracks for demos and smaller clients, were being completed with fewer residual payments to real people. As digital equipment got smaller and more sophisticated, the internet and broadband technology were opening up a whole new level of communication for the ad business. The old line, "someday you might be able to phone in your part," was no longer a joke. It was happening every day. One music house producer described a singer who had made the investment to install a small recording studio in her home: *she didn't want to leave her kids to go to work, so if we wanted her unique solo voice, we e-mailed her the track, she recorded it in her closet with a high-quality microphone, e-mailed it back, got agency comments, then resang it as often as necessary.* No one knows what she looked like, but she sure sounded great.

Jobs that were once awarded only after a *live* presentation made on a piano at the ad agency were being sent out for bids via the internet. For background scores, film edits are posted on the ad agency website; the composer is given a password to download the picture; he syncs it to his sequencing program, does his genius, and delivers an air-quality demo back to the agency by e-mail the next day. Or overnight. Or the files are sent through cyberspace via MP3 from an FTP site or an AIFF file from an E-I-E-I-O site—forget about the password.

Competition was no longer around the corner; it was literally around the world. One colleague said: "There are so many music houses out there, that to get a chance to write a commercial and make any profit from it is only slightly worse than winning the lottery. Agencies have forgotten about, or chosen to ignore, the expense of maintaining a broadcast-quality recording facility. They think all those sounds come free."

Composers from other branches of the music business who

once regarded advertising as a stopgap source of quick income between their regular jobs had become the aggressive competition for the full-time regulars. But the composer was no longer made to feel part of the creative team. Agencies rarely committed to a single supplier without holding a competition for a job. One agency music director interviewed had recently hired music houses in New York, Amsterdam, Munich, and Australia to provide demo tracks for a car commercial. The submission from Australia was a problem, "because of the time zone thing." In some future world, demos will probably come from Mars: guaranteed that the Martians will sign the standard agency music contract, but they probably won't work for scale.

The ad agencies themselves were globalizing: where once there were names of creative giants on the door—Wells Rich Greene; Doyle Dane Bernbach, Ally & Gargano, echoes of a business long gone—now agencies were becoming divisions of mammoth international holding companies, with names alphabetically reduced to confuse everyone except their stockholders. It's unlikely that the CEO of the LMNOP Advertising Agency Conglomerate-Worldwide has any idea who provides the music tracks for the commercials that pay for his round-the-clock limo service.

Another subtle twist of technology was having an enormous impact: in the documentary motion picture *Looking for Richard*, actors Al Pacino and John Gielgud talk about how powerful a tool *silence* is, commenting that nothing commands attention like that special dramatic moment when no one says anything; a chance for a thought to register before the next one comes thundering out to fill the void. In the days when commercials were broadcast on film, the soundtrack for a 60-second TV spot was 58½ seconds long; a 30-second spot had only 28½ seconds of audio. The difference was caused by the "pull-up," the physical distance on the film projector between the sound head and the picture head. When video tape became the standard, no pull-up was necessary, and the old 28½-second track became a full thirty seconds. One-and-a-half seconds may not sound like much, but without it the silence between messages was lost. Now, one commercial began immediately as the preceding spot ended. Butt-to-butt. Instantly. The noise level never stopped. The viewer's thought process had no chance to breathe; and a pod of six 30-second spots had become a nonstop onslaught of audio blur.

Film editors were using computers to shape their commercials—no more chopping block and then taping splices together. An editor who wanted his cut to look good began with a "temp track" to create a mood. Instead of waiting for a traditional custom-made music score to be tailored to the film after-the-fact, it was more fun to work with a pop-record—vocal or instrumental—or the even the introduction to a pop-record, looped to repeat over and over. The unlimited choices of music were now as close as the nearest CD store or internet connection, or the personal tastes of anyone in the project who knew of an obscure a piece of music they wanted to transform into a commercial. It was only a matter of time before everyone came to love whatever it was that they were hearing. Next, everyone agreed that the picture would look better if it was shown to the client along with the temp track. Then: *Why wait and create an original score? We love what we have. And why spend all that money on production when we might be able to get the rights to the actual recording?*

The hunter was loading his rifle.

CD sales had been crippled by digital copying, downloading, and internet piracy, but the uses of pop songs in advertising were giving the record business a huge new breath of life. One music director described how, in 2000, when Sting's latest album sales were flat, his manager hit on the idea of sending the footage from Sting's MTV video to Jaguar's advertising agency, Ogilvy & Mather. In the video, Sting is seen seated in and driving a Jaguar and his manager offered the footage to Jaguar *free* if they would use it in their commercials. In three days time, a 30-second TV spot had been cut, and the rest is history. Sales of both the record and the car took off.

The hunter's target was clearly in sight.

When pop-song music publishers recognized how lucrative advertising music could be, they seized the opportunity and started to actively pitch their catalogs to ad agencies. Record companies, aligning with publishers, formed "creative resource departments," whose sole purpose was to pursue placing their artists and songs into commercials. If a sponsor thought kindly of a song, it might pay millions for sync rights, and then spend millions more in airtime to make it a hit. When an agency wanted the Big Three—the rights from the song's music publisher; the rights from the company that owned the recording; and the rights from the artist who sang the song—the process could almost be one-stop shopping.

All publishers had to do was convince the agencies that using pop songs would make their commercials look *real*; and that a 30-second spot would no longer be a *commercial*; that it would be a thirty-second *film*, scored with an honest-to-goodness pop song, just like in the movies. *The Big Chill* (1983) had been a landmark motion picture, due in large part to the use of actual recordings of pop songs in its sound track. When Marvin Gaye's "I Heard It Through the Grapevine" came blaring out over the opening credits, it had changed the perception of film scoring forever. To the generation of advertising creative types who were brought up on MTV, advertising would no longer be the just the stepchild of art, but now could be art itself.

It was an amazingly easy sell. The agencies already liked the pop-songs-in-commercials idea—film editors had made that possible. Yes, the musicians and singers on the records still had to be paid scale through their unions, but now it was cut-and-dry: there would be no more dickering about how many names would appear on the contracts. "You liked it? You bought it" became the rage.

The ducks were all in a row.

The clients were fed up with production budgets for custom-made music tracks. Studio charges were climbing along with what seemed the daily advancement in new cutting-edge equipment that every agency wanted to use; the jingle house quest for vocal residuals was continuing unchecked; music producers were endlessly seeking multi-payment musicians' residuals even though technology had offered their agency clients a way to lessen the costs.

The hunter was squeezing the trigger.

When pop-music publishers and the newly conjoined record company conglomerates realized that they could offer their songs at a competitive price with custom-made tracks—and still make a fortune—the advertising industry had finally become the marketing arm of the record business.

At that point they had effectively eliminated the custom-made jingle market.

Chapter 9

The Way It Is Today

Nobody thinks anymore.

A copywriter goes to Lyrics.com, types in a category, and gains immediate access to hundreds of song titles, providing not only music ideas for his commercial, but a possible campaign slogan as well.

An art director sifts through the piles of CDs that arrive each day from record labels touting their new and upcoming releases, and searches their covers for inspiration.

An agency producer instructs his film editor to use a particular pop song; *do the cut first and we'll deal with the rights issues later*.

When the smoke had cleared, a new generation of composer/suppliers was providing music for commercials; people with little knowledge of the world that had come before them. A few defiant old timers were still hanging on, senior citizens trying to adapt. One composer-singer colleague from my era said, "Thank God for early retirement benefits!" He was right:

the battle to be listed on the union contracts that had brought about the demise of the jingle business was now paying off— a union pension was providing the majority of his income.

Music publishers, once only bystanders on the fringes of the advertising world were finally in the cat-bird seat, gloating over all the money they were making from the agencies. But the love affair was only temporary. Much like the jingle suppliers before them who believed that their product was indispensable, few publishers understood or cared about the economic differences between a national network sponsor and a regional retailer who wanted to license a song for a four-week holiday promotion. *Hey, it's advertising, right? Advertisers always have lots of money!*

A new way of doing business was taking shape. At first, agencies sought exclusive advertising licenses from publishers to use a particular pop song in a commercial; but when the publishers made that cost astronomically high, full exclusivity became, by default, unnecessary. Advertisers would have to be satisfied with exclusivity within their own product "category." But, shouldn't it matter if the same song is used by different products? Amazingly, it didn't. "My Way," recently appeared in eBay commercials, Mercedes Benz commercials, and for an insurance company (too much "My Way" to remember which one), all at the same time! When I questioned an agency music director about the fact that his hotel chain was using the same pop song as a cosmetic product, he ducked the subject, taking the myopic view that as long as his client was happy, it didn't matter. "It's a Wonderful World" has been used in so many different commercials that the only product identity it leaves is that it's a wonderful song.

Sometimes, production schedules got ahead of sensibility. If a film edit was completed before the agency investigated the cost of obtaining rights to their pop-song "temp track," getting a price after-the-fact became a tricky process. Naturally, in order to keep the license fee down, an inventive agency business manager would try not to reveal the name of the product in his inquiry. A music publisher who heard that his song was under consideration by a national advertiser also heard the soft purring engine of his new Porsche and the gentle caress of the waves in front of his summer rental on Nantucket.

The more money publishers sought to squeeze out of advertisers, the larger the legal difficulties became for the full- . time music supplier.

A sponsor who could only afford to buy the rights to the song (and not the artist or the record) might hire a music house to do a rearrangement, perhaps using a girl's voice instead of the man who was on the hit record, all with the careful intent of not being accused of stealing the *sound* of the pop artist or the recording. So far, so good: arranging fees could pay a music supplier's rent.

But when any, or all of the Big Three was unobtainable, whether due to price or just the agency's desire to try and get away with something—the nobody-will-ever-find-out-that-the-spot-was-broadcast-in-Idaho mentality—the music house was told, "Use this pop song as a guide, as a reference: give us something like it; close-enough, but make sure we don't get sued." A new category of advertising music was born: the pop tune *knock-off*.

We live in a litigious society. Today, anybody can and will sue anybody for anything. Handling accusatory letters and phone calls are standard agency business. There are always quacks and cranks ready to jump on the bandwagon of a successful advertising campaign. All they need is a lawyer willing to work on a contingency basis—sharks drool to be involved in music-business cases.

A few years ago I received a phone call from an attorney who represented a ventriloquist who was suing Pepsi Cola. He had heard that I had some experience in defending the misuses of my copyrights and wanted some advice. It seems that his client had appeared at a nightclub in the same city as a Pepsi Bottler Convention, and a part of his usual act included a routine where his dummy answered questions by saying "uh huh" to everything. Shortly thereafter, Diet Pepsi began using a jingle, performed by Ray Charles and The Raylettes, called "You Got the Right One Baby, Uh huh." The ventriloquist was claiming that his "uh huh" had been stolen. The lawyer had already filed papers with the court, and wanted to know my thoughts about how much to seek if a settlement was proposed. I suggested that since he would certainly have to prove that his "Uh huh" was completely original and proprietary to his ventriloquist before he would be able to show that Diet Pepsi had copied it; and since the campaign will be probably be off the air long before the lawsuit reached a courtroom, if they offered him a case of Diet Pepsi, to take it. Even a six-pack. Uh huh! (P.S., the case was dismissed.)

To complicate the music supplier's life even further, believe it or not, there is a company out there today that specializes in the Gestapo tactic of monitoring broadcasts, listening to commercials, and then alerting music publishers that their songs have been ripped off by advertisers. For a fee, of course

A claim that never reaches a trial can still end up costing lots of money. The agencies all carry their own insurance coverage, as do their individual clients. But in order to reduce their premiums, they have chosen to include very high deductibles, often $100,000 to $200,000. Now, when a settlement is reached in that bang-bang lawsuit brought by a music publisher against an advertiser, the deductible amount must be paid by the agency *before* their insurance kicks in. Agency stockholders didn't like this business expense being taken from their bottom-line profit. So what happened? Some smart lawyer said: "Let's pass the buck to the music houses. They never say, 'No.'"

The result? Today, most agencies insist that their music suppliers carry "errors-and-omissions" insurance or they will not even be considered for work. The premium for an insurance policy with a million-dollar coverage—the latest agency minimum requirement—costs $7,500 to $10,000 per year, an expense that must be *borne by the music supplier*.

Once again, the music house is caught in the middle, forced to assume legal liability for the ad agency's lack of imagination, putting itself first in line of defense against lawsuits from music publishers or recording artists or record companies whose materials it was just instructed to rip-off by the agency!

As usual, the music houses never say "no."

But it's not that simple. The insurance companies got wise to the ad agency policy of avoiding responsibility: insurers are now insisting that a "forensic" musicologist's report be written immediately after the creation of the job, providing a expert opinion about the originality of the music. (Can you imagine the word "forensic" being used in a business that supplies music for fried chicken?) In some cases, originality means how close a rearrangement came to the record version that the client refused to buy and instructed the music supplier to imitate! The punch line? Without this formal report, the music house's insurance will not be effective.

A simple musicologist's opinion costs $300 to $500. Guess who is expected to pay for the report? New items have begun to appear on music house invoices: the *download* item (the sushi-lunch); the *upload-download* item (the client-limo); and the *backload-reload* item (the musicologist's report). If the work was for McDonalds, do they call it a "McLoad?"

In their own gentle-but-desperate way, music production houses are trying to adapt to the new pop-song mentality. One still-in-there-but-barely jingle composer described himself as "the mini-me of 1970." Some music houses are making their *own* alliances with record companies to help them market their songs—for a fee, of course—and get them into ads. Now, when a job opportunity is received by the music house, the first thing that happens is not the suggestion of an original music approach, but . . . *does anyone know any pop songs that might fit the needs of this project? Or something even more obscure and cutting-edge?* It's a matter of survival, doing everything and anything to win a job and stay in business.

Music houses are also offering "retreads," to ad agencies, compilations of their own rejected demos. With everything infinitely re-editable, why not float some of the unselected gems out there with a new coat of paint, sans lyric, and license *them* as original music for ads? If a spot is cut to a retread, a client might come to love it! Retreads are often sent on CDs to film editors, in categories: *What do you need? Soft rock? Hard rock? Rap? Hip Hop? Punk?*

Talk about being inventive: one music house interviewed had even created a fictitious rock group, and was peddling it to ad agencies as one of the latest hot/new/edgy *underground* sounds, on an *underground* record label (their own, of course).

In a competition, multiple demos have become the norm. Each music house invariably submits four or five demo tracks, sometimes written by four or five different individuals. Imagine: twenty-plus approaches developed by each suitor in a competition. All with no additional compensation!

An agency business affairs manager told me: "Advertising agencies and their clients have never been in as strong and dominating position over the entire music industry in general and the advertising music business supplier specifically, as they are today."

For the music house, the ownership of rights and copy-rights has never been of less importance. One of the questions I asked every person I interviewed was: "If you were to write a novel, or a popular song, or a screenplay, or the plot for a sit-com, or the script for a theatre piece—all those creative works that are considered *intellectual property*, whose potential income could last as long as copyright protection allowed, your lifetime-plus-seventy-years—would you sell those rights for a one-time fee?"

Music producers all responded they would like to improve their collective lot, but that they simply can't afford to risk offending clients by raising thorny business issues that are contrary to the status quo. Everyone knows that there are lines and lines of music suppliers waiting on the end of their modems, ready to do anything—and sign anything—just to get a foot in the door. No one is willing to take a stand strong enough to try to change the system. But everyone would certainly like someone else to do it for them. One colleague summed it up quite accurately: "Today, every music house has a man with a mortgage."

Progress comes with the ability to have choices, and today there are few choices available. In recent years, a new advertising industry trade group, the Association of Music Producers (AMP) has been formed. Much like the old SAMPAC, AMP has lofty goals: seminars have been held with agency business managers, lawyers, and musicologists to enlighten both sides about the legal problems created by the rampant use of temp tracks by film editors; and which party should be responsible when problems arise. But no one dares stand up to try and change the system, either individually or collectively.

In the beginning of my career, I paid no attention to the clause in the standard agency music contract wherein the composer agrees to offer an *unlimited* indemnification against any *alleged* breach of contract, even though all the ideas and direction for the music (and often the lyrics) had been provided by the advertising agency. I asked colleagues how they felt about being put into this vulnerable position; everyone said that they never questioned it—that it was just *standard*.

I called an insurance broker, who found a company that

offered an errors-and-omissions policy that would extend to the music business. The premium was $350 a year (then) for a policy that would provide $100,000 to $300,000 worth of liability coverage, much like car insurance. I decided it was worth this minimal business expense because film editors were beginning to use pop records to show agency producers how wonderful their work was, and there was potential danger lurking in every editing suite. Why not sleep at night? But after a few years of this modest cost, suddenly my premium jumped, for no reason, from $350 a year to $3,500 a year, a *one-thousand-percent* increase! I questioned my insurance broker, who told me that medical doctors were being sued more and more by patients for malpractice and that errors-and-omissions policies as a general category were becoming more expensive. I decided to examine other alternatives.

I learned first that legal battles in the music business rarely reach a courtroom. Everyone yells and screams in the beginning, and expensive lawyers file expensive documents and conduct expensive pre-trial discovery. Later, after everyone gets tired of yelling and screaming, the inevitable settlement is reached, and the lawyers work it out so that one of insured parties pays the settlement. (As a sidebar, for the music house, what is known in legal parlance as "reasonable attorney fees" is usually measured in staggeringly large amounts, especially when compared with creative and arranging fees.)

It became clear that the only reason the music house was expected to put themselves on the frontline was because the music house allowed it! What made the most sense to me was to acknowledge the collaborative nature of the advertising business, and to limit the amount of my liability to the fair dollar value of the creative fee I had been paid; and then make the indemnification effective only after a *proven* breach—a decision reached in a court of law, and not a settlement agreed to at the convenience of others. By doing that, I would effectively be insuring myself.

I had an attorney draft that concept into language that I put in my contract form. From that day on, I never worked without it. Agency lawyers, without exception, hated that clause. "Aren't you proud enough of your originality to stand behind it?" was the most-often heard remark. "I stand completely behind my originality to the extent of the amount you paid for it, but this is not an I-love-you song that grew out of my own creativity. I work at *your* direction. And by the way, do you indemnify your clients against an incorrect legal opinion?"

When I described some of my own struggles and goals to one of the young interviewees for this book, she commented: "Those things all sound wonderful, but what are you getting so worked up about? It's only advertising!"

My response: "How can you do your best work unless you really care about it? If you don't have some level of respect for what you do from morning to night, how are you ever going to improve your working conditions?"

Everyone likes to hear about the nuts and bolts of how much money is earned, and how it is spent in music production. The public perceives that a jingle composer (aka, the modern music supplier) enjoys a cushy life of fun, games, and Chateau Petrus. America, it just ain't so. What follows is a careful consensus, weeding out the anxiety that this subject raised in every interview, which describes the rest of today's dollar story.

DEMO FEES

Typical demo fees average $1,500, or whatever is agreed to in the we-don't-have-a-lot-of-money-at-this-stage phone call. Most often agencies will pay for demos. Sometimes they won't—if they can get away with it. Nothing is quite as heroic as an agency producer taking bows after convincing a music house to provide a free demo.

Years ago, I had written the music for the local CBS radio station in New York City. It was played each quarter-hour to introduce the news, sports, weather, and entertainment segments, and had run for almost ten years. When they did a thirtieth-anniversary program and broadcast it again, I received a call from the new station manager. "There was great public reaction to the old music. We'd like to update it. Do you work on spec?"

"No," I replied. "Do you?"

Silence. He didn't like that.

The majority of the demo fee is allocated for ongoing operating costs: rent, telephone, electricity, etc., and for keeping up with the latest cutting-edge electronic machines that are a standard part of the music house's facility. Sometimes, the equipment is owned outright by the music house for use by anyone working on a project; sometimes, it's owned by the independent composer who is given a room to park his gear so he can be available to work (usually for free) at a moments notice.

Keeping other demo costs at a minimum is a must.

If necessary, freelance musicians are hired to augment the machines, although in-house composers, arrangers, or engineers (today, everyone is an engineer of sorts) who also can play guitar, bass, drums, or keyboards are preferable, because they will not have to be paid for that service. One music house stressed that a *guitar*-playing composer-arranger is more in demand than a *keyboard*-playing composer, making one less outside player to hire during the demo process.

Any singers that are needed will also be the in-house employees who will not have to be paid—composers and arrangers will often sing the solo parts, and also *double* in the background group. Sometimes, there is a need for that special freelance singer with a unique cutting-edge sound who must be paid. (Remember that lady who phones in her part? Maybe she really looks like Jennifer Aniston. Maybe she looks like Señor Wences' fist.) There are some music houses who define "freelance" singers as those who will gladly come to work for nothing on the demo, just for the honor of the *potential* of getting on the union contract if, as, and when the demo becomes a final.

The issue of how much a musician or a singer was paid for a demo evoked the most evasive answers during the interviews for this book. Most producers said they paid "scale" to talent, but did not file any paperwork with the unions, meaning no pension and welfare contributions. (This closely guarded secret "demo scale" ranged from $50 to $100 for both players and singers.) The unions have never trusted the sponsors, and none of them recognizes the concept of "a demo," primarily because they fear that a demo track produced for a lower-than-scale amount might be broadcast out-of-town without the talent ever knowing about it.

In the demo stage, if necessary, a small fee might be paid to a freelance musical arranger who is able to provide a style that no one in the music house can produce.

Out of a $1,500 demo fee, the composer who is not a principal of the music house might receive $200 to $400 for his/her effort, whether it's a demo rearrangement style of an existing pop song (or two or four—all for one price), or the rare creation of a completely new original melody (or three or eight—still all for one price). Music houses often have several novices hanging around just waiting for their big chance, neophytes willing to work for nothing, just for the opportunity to be included in the game and get their music out there. In theory, a good idea; in practice, ultimately unfair—if something comes in, no matter how small, there should be a taste for everyone.

On the other side of that argument, when talking to newcomers, I have always advocated that in the beginning there is no middle—take every job, regardless of the money. Working is the prime goal. You can't eat principle. Once you're established and have learned the ropes, you can start to refine your financial terms. But without a reputation and a track record, all the high-minded goals of achieving a fair deal are meaningless.

WHEN THE DEMO BECOMES A FINAL

Any monies earned and spent during the demo process are gone. After surviving demo-hell, payments to the winning music house start all over again from the beginning, in one of two ways: either with a single lump sum that covers all items of production, leaving the division of the pie up to the discretion of the music house; or in a break-down scenario, where the music house sends an itemized bill which separates creative fee, arranging fee, studio time, etc.

There are advantages to both.

THE CREATIVE FEE

Composer creative fees range from $2,500 to $10,000, averaging $7,500, depending on whether the client is a big national advertiser or a smaller regional one. This is a one-time fee, never to be repeated.

(Yet, under the category of respect, if the advertising agency has hired the Hollywood composer who wrote the score for a current hit movie, the creative fee might be up to $100,000. Advertisers want cutting-edge, and are not afraid to pay for it. Unfortunately, full-time advertising music-production houses today are only thought of only as *conduits* of cutting-edge, not creators, no matter how long they let their hair grow.)

If the composer is a music-house employee, but not a principal, the usual creative-fee split is still 60% to the music house, 40% to the composer (sometimes 70–30; rarely 50–50).

If the composer works for himself or in a partnership, obviously he gets to keep more.

THE ARRANGING FEE

The winning music house will also receive an *arranging fee*, normally between $1,500 and $3,500 per spot, averaging $2,000.

The in-house arranger usually receives 40% of the total arranging fee. Or 30%, or whatever is negotiated, depending on how dark it is in the hallway because someone has been late paying the electric bill.

If the arranger works freelance, he/she might be able to negotiate a slightly larger part of the total arranging fee. But there is normally not a lot of room to wiggle.

STUDIO COSTS

Here's how the music houses pay their rent. When the job becomes a final, a given number of hours are allocated toward studio costs, usually at $350 to $450 per hour. Ten to twenty hours of studio time are billed to the agency, even though it actually took many more to complete the job.

Sometimes the agency will pay additional amounts for revisions they request during the demo process. Sometimes not. There is the continuing ad agency perception that the music house has all that equipment just waiting around, ready and willing to serve.

THE ONE-LUMP BILL

Sometime the agency will say, "We've got $17,000 for the whole job. Can you do it?" The music house may figure a quick estimate, but the answer is always "yes." If actual costs get out of hand during production for some unforeseen reason, a compassionate agency producer may be able to get more from the client. A package of three spots starts to sound like good money.

I don't mean to portray agency employees as heartless cutthroats who are only concerned with the bottom line of production costs, but the fierce competition between music houses has created a working atmosphere where agencies know that music houses are willing to do anything just to land the job. Like it or not, it's reality.

UNION VERSUS NON-UNION

Big-time advertising is a union business, and all the major advertising agencies are signatories to the union talent codes. Some advertisers might want to work non-union but can't because they are heavily involved with other trade unions at their manufacturing plants. Non-union means a "buy-out," a one-time payment to everyone, no residuals, no pension/welfare/health benefits, nothing to anyone ever again, and the sponsor owns the track and can use it forever and ever and ever . . .

Every advertising music producer, with rare exception, is a signatory to the union contracts: SAG, AFTRA, and the AF of M. Once a music house signs the codes, they are honor-bound to comply with union rules, and to provide all the benefits that the unions have won for their members through the years. Singers, musicians, and actors all aspire to union membership because it means recognition as professional craftsmen at the top of their trade. It would seem crazy for anyone—particularly the music houses whose foundation of income depends so much on union-won residuals—to want to work under any other system. Yet, the pressure on music suppliers to produce buy-out work grows as each client's yearly advertising budget shrinks with changing times.

But what if a sponsor can't afford or, for whatever reason, does not wish to allocate money for union scale wages or residuals? Suppose he is willing to pay a music supplier a full creative and arranging fee, one-time only, but asks that the tracks be produced non-union under buy-out conditions? Will the composer be able to sit in his living room without throwing up during every broadcast when his wonderful song enters its ninth year? Comedian Professor Irwin Corey once said that "suicide is the sincerest form of self-criticism."

During the times when there are lots of jobs, and everyone is making lots of money, there is always great support for union principles. But when economic pressures demand that music suppliers and the talent they hire take whatever work is offered—under whatever conditions—the system is weakened. During poor business cycles, working non-union is often more a matter of survival than choice. Union musicians and singers are not permitted to accept non-union commercials, but obviously the talent comes from somewhere, so it's not unreasonable to assume that some folks are AC/DC.

The supplier producing tracks completely by one-man band synthesizer has a tiny but viable avenue of protection in the non-union world. If, say, the local swimming pool builder wants music to advertise with, and offers a one-time "buyout" fee for the creation of an original melody, the composer (or the company he/she forms) can still be a signatory to the AF of M codes, and make payments to himself in full accordance with the union agreements. The swimming pool company does not have to be a signatory to any codes, nor do they care how the money they paid out is used. The music house merely allocates the correct portion of its fee toward union scales, welfare, etc., and files the appropriate paperwork with the union. This greatly benefits the music supplier, because it offers the build-up of union-earned income to qualify for pension and medical coverage. The union welcomes members who work under union conditions, and this is a completely legal opportunity to make payments as if it were a big union job. Even paying quarterly union residuals (to themselves) may be cheaper than carrying an outside medical coverage policy.

There is no such thing as a full-time jingle singer anymore, regardless of how talented. Those who get the work earn less because there is less Class A network use. Advertisers are spending more on cable TV, where residuals are cheaper and there is more bang for their buck. In the dictionary, under "buyout," is a picture of a former jingle singer pumping gas at an Exxon station. In the old days, she might have owned that Exxon station, if she had been smart with her money. But probably not. The overfunded-pension jingle singers from days past who used to maintain numbered Swiss bank accounts, and owned race horses and homes on exotic islands have mostly spent it all—not that living well is a bad thing—but when you're riding the wave, you think it'll never reach the shore. With rare exception, the stars from my era have all readjusted their lifestyles to no longer earning cutting-edge income.

The "no-such-thing" rule applies to studio-musicians as well. For players, the biggest change has been that a sponsor rarely runs the same track for more than one cycle (thirteen weeks), and this has vastly reduced residual income. Adding to the studio players' woes, when the bottom fell out of the record business, it made all those musical stars available to compete for advertising work, thereby limiting even further the number of job opportunities for musicians. In New York, those who once thrived in the jingle business now work in the few Broadway show orchestras. What was once considered "the pits" is now one of the best and most sought-after jobs in town.

There's a telling story about the difficult state of the music business: a parent approaches a professional player, and says: "My son wants to be a musician. What should he do?"

The musician answers: "Buy him a tuxedo, and let him eat standing up in a kitchen for a month. After that, if he still wants to be a musician, buy him an instrument."

Chapter 10

America Has Ads-heimers

People used to say, "The commercials are better than the program."

Not any more.

The public is tuning out the ads.

Ad agencies have bigger budgets per minute for commercial production than most feature movies.

Yet the public is tuning out the ads.

Advertisers are faced with the same problem as a parent who screams in frustration that her kids aren't listening to her: the more the parent yells at the kid to keep his room clean, the dirtier it gets. Mama's words have lost their punch. Even Mama's punch has lost its effectiveness, because the kid knows he will survive it. Advertising people are less believable today than car salesmen and politicians.

More and more, consumers cannot identify the product in their recall of a commercial, and if they do remember the commercial at all they might tell you something about it, but they can't connect that information with a sponsor. That's because nobody is singing about the *product*. The pop songs in commercials are singing about everything *but* the product.

There used to be a music business here, but the giant advertising agency holding companies tore down the jingle jungle and built condos. Not even solid, well-designed, well-thought-out comfortable places for sale, to own and to build equity in; but small rooms with cardboard walls for rent only to short-term tenants who'll pay for the space with short-term ideas destined to be bombarded on a public with an even shorter memory span.

Ads have become sneaky, pretending to entertain—*we'll give them a joke and then slip the sponsor's name in at the end in a product shot.* But, for the first twenty seconds of a spot, the consumer doesn't even know the name of the product.

And by then, who cares?

Advertising is cockroaches, and people are waiting with a shoe in their hand, and when commercials come on they smack them out, they TiVo them out, they zap them out; or they simply get up and walk out of the room. And even if they stay in the room, they effectively tune out the ads because commercials don't sound like advertising. They sound like everything *but* advertising.

When did it become wrong to *sell* something? What's wrong with selling? Producing a great product and marketing it is the idea that made America great.

Who killed the jingle?

Frightened people who have forgotten what business they are in, and what they are being paid to do: to communicate a message to their audience *about a product!*

People who are afraid to take a chance on a tried and tested tool, so instead they take the hip new flavor-of-the-moment and recycle something that was created for something else, and hope the day ends quickly. And then it's on to the next recycle to get through the next day.

Music suppliers are in big trouble because agencies don't want to have anything to do with anyone who has anything to do with advertising.

Advertisers have forgotten what it takes to be first at something; forgotten that their job is to establish a unique selling position and audio platform for their product and then stick with it and not run away from it when it hits the first inevitable bump.

But everyone can sure tell you what's wrong. The ad columns and trade papers are filled with complaining galore:

"Advertising is dumb. Movies have gotten dumb. TV has gotten dumb. Advertisers are saying implicitly that their consumers are dumb. We are catering to the lowest common denominator out there and by doing that we are creating it. Advertising is creating stupid people, blasting viewers with vulgarity, with sleazy commercials, with sophomoric humor, with punch lines centered on bodily functions, violence, and double entendre. The 30-second spot is dead. Ads don't appeal to the best in human nature. They appeal to the worst in us. There is a new generation of teenagers for whom television is little more than background noise."

One radio network worries that because so many commercials are broadcast, the messages are being diluted. "Don't touch that dial; we'll be right back," has become an automatic call for the consumer to change stations.

Madison Avenue is desperate to find a way to reach an audience. The advertising industry has produced study after study, ad nauseam, with information about how viewership of TV network programming is dropping; how sponsors are spending their dollars elsewhere, struggling to reach a market, *any* market; how the networks are charging more for airtime while they deliver a smaller audience each year. Everyone blames the fragmented media for the lack of sponsor impact, but no one ever steps up to the plate and blames the content of the commercial. "There's nothing wrong with the spots," they say, "we just have to find a way to get them heard!"

Bull! If the ads were better, people would pay more attention!

The commercials broadcast on Super Bowl XXXVIII made headlines when Justin Timberlake ripped off Janet Jackson's bra-top. Without that "costume malfunction," the spots might have been once-noted on the ad pages, and then forgotten, but the resulting publicity highlighted much more than poor Janet's pasty. For an instant, America was focused on the taste-less quality of the creative ideas. But then it was back to business as usual.

A recent column in *Ad Week* magazine carried the head-line, "Since When Does a Popular Song Pass as Creativity?" Yet, there are never columns about how to *fix* a problem.

OK, here's a thought that might be considered in the holding company boardrooms: maybe if corporations worry a little less about the bottom line and a little more about the *content* of the ads, the public would remember them more, and actually *like* their advertising and then buy their products or services.

There is no reason a jingle cannot be produced with a cutting-edge sound. But the lyric has to be *about the product*, and not be afraid to actually name it, or the ad that costs mil-lions to produce and broadcast fails.

Right now, I know someone is saying, "Steve, you can't fix every problem with a jingle!" But what's out there now is sure-ly not working, so it's certainly worth a serious try. It's worked before!

The spots that we remember through the years are the ones that *sang* to us about the product, or *danced* for us about the product, or entertained us *musically* about the product for thirty seconds, and we in turn would always watch, because original custom-made advertising music demanded our atten-tion; and when you went to the store and saw the product, you remembered the jingle! There was a time when seasonal commercials meant Christmas was coming, just like there was a time when people called their children into the room to listen to the President.

Sure, every once in a while a courageous advertiser lets a jingle creep through the cracks, but the big guys—the cars, the burgers, the beers—are nowhere in the ballpark. And yes, occasionally, there is a custom-made vocal tag line at the end of a ton of announcer copy, but rarely is the entire advertiser's message ever told in full lyrics, something the public can remember, something that takes a little time to sink in, something that won't be tuned out. Commercial content ought to be more than just a sound-byte. When the message is *only* in the five-second tag, the other twenty-five seconds are thrown away.

Ask anyone over thirty what's in a Big Mac, and they will tell you: "Two all-beef patties, special sauce, lettuce, cheese, pickles, onions on a sesame seed bun." That's because it was *sung*.

In the futuristic movie *Demolition Man*, Sylvester Stallone and Sandra Bullock are police officers. As they drive around in their jet powered-patrol car, they laugh and sing the latest hottest music craze of that era—classic jingles!

Quality never goes out of style.

Custom-made music and lyrics for advertising are quality. Using pop songs instead exhibits nothing more than a profound lack of imagination. People don't resent all commercials; they resent bad ones.

Unless advertising returns to *selling*, people will continue to turn it off. The answer is not to eliminate commercials or to find new ways of sneaking them into our lives (like putting ads on people's cell phones or making them a hateful part of the previews at the local movie house), but to go back and make advertising what it once was. Honest. And entertaining.

Years ago, David Ogilvy, founder of Ogilvy and Mather Advertising said, "If you have nothing to say, sing it." Today's corollary is, "If you have something to say, and want it *remembered*, sing it!"

People still don't hum the announcer, and they never will.

Here's one I'd love to see:
It's Sunday night.

I turn on my TV to watch *60 Minutes*, and it's time for Andy Rooney.

> "Remember when commercials sang to you?
> [Andy sings]
> *'Pepsi-cola hits the spot...'*
> *'Use Ajax, boom boom, the foaming cleanser...'*
> *'We are the men from Texaco; we work from Maine to Mexico . . . '*
> Now, you know I'm not much of a singer, but those words and their cute little melodies stuck in your head, sometimes for years. They were *jingles*—that's what they called them—that someone wrote and someone sang just to get you to remember their beer, or car or cola.
> Those jingles were part of American culture, and there was a tacit agreement between the television viewer and the sponsor: 'I'll listen to your little song 'cause it pays for the show I like, rather than have the whole show bastardized by products turning up all over the place 'in the show.'
> [Andy whispers]
> In the business, they call that 'integration'—where the whole damn program is saturated with people eating and drinking and driving and holding and standing in front of and sitting on top of the . . . 'Paid Promotional Sponsor.'
> [Back to full voice]

People don't like commercials today. Oh, they may laugh once, but the second time the flatulent horse comes on, they reach for the zapper. And the background music has diddly-squat to do with whatever the product is. I hear an old song in a commercial, and I don't remember what they're selling 'cause it has nothing to do with what they're selling! But it sure makes me think about my old high school girlfriend, and . . . well, that's another subject.

Hey, Madison Avenue: wanna win me back? I'll watch your 30-second spot as long as I *like* it!'

I say, 'Bring back the Clydesdales in the snow.' 'Here Comes the King' made me wait for the spot to be over *before* I went to the frig for a beer.

I'll watch your spots again.

Just sing to me.

[sings]

'When You Say Budweiser, You've Said It All.'"

Be my guest, Andy. Anytime you like.

Chapter 11

How I Got Out

recently found the following message on my voice mail:

"Hi, Steve, I'm calling from DDB-Needham Advertising. We're handling the commercials for the New York State lottery, and there's going to be a version called the 'I Love New York' game. We've spoken with the Department of Economic Development and gotten permission to use the music. We know your *father* wrote the song, and we're wondering if you know where the tapes are? Please call me at . . . "

That's a true story.

I've always believed that a music house has to have one big hit a year to remain on top. For a long time, I enjoyed my share of milestones and was able to achieve that goal. I also made cutting-edge business progress by licensing my jingles; retaining copyright ownership; earning residuals for their uses; limiting my indemnification; and keeping the ability to collect ASCAP performances and all the non-advertising income earned by my music. (Please see Chapter Four: "How I Got Smart.")

By 1990, advertising agency attitudes were changing as fast as technology, and it had become harder and harder to sell my deal.

And I wouldn't work without it.

I couldn't.

Whenever I have one of those Barbara Walters fantasies— I'm her guest on the program that precedes the Academy Awards and she asks one of those Barbara Walters–type questions—I imagine she says: "Steve, what's your favorite word?"

My answer is easy.

Honor.

I had given my word. To my industry and to myself. Finish what you commit to do, and accept nothing less from others.

Advertising is the world's biggest popularity contest, and after a twenty-five-year career, though there were still some in the new generation of agency producers that wanted to work with me, their business departments wouldn't buy my terms or accept my contract form. For the first time, I hired a sales rep. I had never needed one before. He ran around with my reel for three months. Everyone was impressed, but he couldn't sell my deal. Copyright ownership? Indemnification clauses? It was like talking Greek.

Friends urged me to give in, so I could keep writing. *Sign the standard agency music agreement! Everyone else does.*

That was the problem: everyone else did.

For me, it would have been a step backwards.

I live an hour away from Manhattan and I never opened an office or recording facility in the City, to be in the middle of the action. I did put a MIDI-studio in my home, and started to turn out some pretty good demos. But every job opportunity had become a competition. For me, the constant demo process removed the *passion* factor, the feeling of pride in a job that separates good from great. The business was no longer fun. The industry had become more about winning than writing great music.

Comedians tell jokes in threes. Whatever the subject, it's a setup, a build, and then the punch line. Watch Leno or Letterman; it's always three in a row; the topic is planted, caressed, and you're hooked.

Three men are in a bar, and the first says . . . and the second says . . . and the third . . . bam!

A priest, a minister, and a rabbi are on an airplane, discussing when life begins, and the priest says . . .

A Frenchman, an Italian, and an American are bragging about how they make their women scream during sex, and the Frenchman says . . .

I've discussed this phenomenon with friends who are professional comedians and one thing is certain: three works; four is too much. You might not recognize the first as the start of a three, but with a little experience, pretty soon you can see what's coming. A shrink once told me, "*The* first time something happens it's an accident; the second time it's suspicious; the third time it's a pattern."

For me when it got to three, it was over.

One.

I was in the middle of a session for Continental Airlines, and on a break, I had a chance to chat with my young agency producer. She had recently graduated from the Newhouse School of Communications at Syracuse University. "Oh, my daughter went there, too," I said proudly.

From that moment on, it was icicles. It was clear that she didn't like the idea of working with someone her father's age.

In advertising, they don't want one fifty; they want two twenty-fives.

Two.

I was slugging through demo-hell with a client who inquired about my new MIDI-studio. "Which keyboard do you use?" he asked.

"A Korg M-1," I said, hoping to impress with the then cutting-edge piece of equipment I'd bought to stay current in the game.

"Oh," my client smiled coyly, "I just bought one of those for my twelve-year-old son."

When a twelve-year-old kid can produce the same sounds as a twenty-five-year pro, it's a sign.

Three.

I had won the Hertz account for Wells Rich Greene Advertising. I know my song was responsible for winning the business because I was told by the exuberant agency CEO that the client had stopped the presentation in the middle of the pitch after hearing "Hertz, We're America's Wheels," and awarded them the account right there. As was typical, for a few years, I did all the rearrangements for radio and TV. One day, there was a new head of Hertzdom, who decided that an animated commercial would be cute and different. This new client rep wanted to have several music houses *compete* for the rearrangement job. "If you want a shot at it, you have to do it, a $1,500 demo," I was told by my long-time friends at the agency.

I got a copy of the film from the animator, recorded a neat little track in my home-studio, using my by-then well-known melody, and submitted it.

They chose someone else's version.

My contract insured that my company would continue to receive residuals while they ran the animated spot—and all the other commercials they produced during the rest of the campaign that I was not a part of—until Wells Rich Greene went out of business and the account changed agencies and slogans.

The notes were on the wall. 1-2-3.

1) The business was being run by a generation who instinctively wanted to work with those more of their own age;

2) Cutting-edge equipment could be bought by anyone with $798;

3) Clients were unshakeable in demo-land.

I have always admired athletes and performers who were able to keep their ego in control enough to know when it was time to do a polite fade.

For me, that time had come.

That's when I quit.

Epilogue

In the years that followed, I wrote only one advertising campaign, for a friend's agency, to promote the annual Radio City Music Hall Christmas show. My music is now entering its eighth year, and recently scored in the top ten percent of all commercials ever tested by a particular major research company for memorability and clarity of message delivery. I also did some pro bono work for the Greater New York Hospital Association: one commercial (with full lyrics) to fight governmental cuts in the Medicare and Medicaid Programs; another (with full lyrics) designed to increase Congressional awareness about how many people don't have and can't afford medical insurance. These were interesting, challenging jobs, no competitions, strictly creative, the way it's supposed to be.

It took a while to steer the battleship into a new direction, but there were many pluses to moving on. I completed a memoir about my early days in show business and growing up with my high school pal, Bobby Darin. It was one of those wonderfully pleasurable someday-when-I-have-the-time projects. The hardcover version of *Me and Bobby D.* was published in 2003, and I'm proud that it's now in paperback.

I write songs for my grandchildren, for my daughters' weddings, and for special friends who are celebrating major birthdays and anniversaries, all joyous effort, and not at all like work.

I'm close to the end of composing a musical. (Doesn't everyone know someone who is writing a musical?) One supportive life-long buddy keeps bugging me to finish it, saying that it had better open on Broadway before they need to construct a ramp to get his wheel chair into the theatre. I'm doing my best to keep him healthy.

I've never felt more comfortable in my creative skin. My work days are just as long as they ever were—there are never enough hours—but now redirected towards more substantive subject matter. A deadline is still the ultimate inspiration, even though it is now self-imposed. Maybe it was always that way.

The ASCAP issue remains the hardest to let go. I often have to step back from the urge to dash out a letter-to-the-editor against some ASCAP-sponsored activity that would further solidify their stranglehold on the music industry. I cracked a few years ago and wrote to members of Congress arguing against ASCAP's then-latest attempt to extend the copyright law. On the surface, extension sounded like a good thing for all songwriters, but in reality it would only have continued the current unchangeable distribution system for yet another twenty years. Of course, the law passed anyway, and months later I received cordial, generic responses from some of the Senators I had written to, assuring me that my opinion would be carefully considered when the matter came up for a vote. I'm back to trying not to send letters.

Writing *Who Killed the Jingle?* allowed me a positive reflection on twenty-five years of my life. As stated earlier, I had a great run, and it's been a rewarding experience to be able to put in all in perspective.

Some of my jingles are still on the air, but most have been replaced by pop-songs or slice-of-life comedy vignettes that are currently perceived as more cutting-edge.

There's one final story that adds a perfect postscript to this book.

I recently received a call from a friend to inform me that he had just heard a new commercial using one of my major hits from the 1980s, "Trust the Midas Touch," on a network-TV sporting event.

A few days later, someone from the business affairs department of Midas' advertising agency called to say that their new client had decided to go back to my jingle because it provided the best consumer identification their products have had during the last twenty years. And, because I owned the copyright, I was entitled to payment.

But there was a problem: Midas could not afford residuals, at least not at the level called for in our contract. If we could not negotiate a discounted rate, Midas would be unable to continue to use the music. Would I agree to a one-time fee for a year's unlimited use?

Though it was to be for a fraction of our contractual deal, I said "Yes." It would be a substantiation of everything I wrote about in this book: that the irrelevant pop-songs that had been used in the interim had not been as effective for Midas as their own instantly recognizable jingle.

Another call: Would I make it a two-year deal?

No problem.

Another call: Midas would like to make it a five-year deal.

No problem.

The next call: Please send an invoice to the agency.

Done.

The next: Please redo the invoice and send it directly to Midas.

No problem.

Then, silence.

When I hadn't heard from anyone for a few weeks, not even a "the check is in the mail" phone call, I contacted the agency. *The client is traveling, it's all a done deal, nothing to worry about, and it will be wrapped up soon.* A month went by as I continued to hear my song on TV.

One day, the agency faxed a cute *amendment* to my contract, prepared by the Midas lawyer, which completely altered the terms of our existing twenty-two year-old agreement. If I had signed it they would own everything including the key lyric, which I had protected with twenty-seven copyrights on all the versions and rearrangements I had produced. More importantly, it would also mean that after they paid the fee for the first year they would have the right to commission a different song using my lyric, and thereby avoid all future payments. The amendment also tried to unlimit my limited indemnification, plus a few other gems I will not waste time or paper to describe.

Of course, I said no to everything, and put Midas on notice that if they didn't pay for the first year's use by a certain date, our good faith reduced-rate offer would expire.

At the exact hour of expiration, the agency business manager called and asked me not to revoke the license using the thirty-day breach-of-contract clause in our agreement—not, at least, until I talked directly with Midas's representative.

I'm expecting the call tomorrow, so I can't inform you of the result of that conversation. But, there is no question in my mind and heart that I will defend my contract and copyrights to whatever extent is necessary.

I describe the details of this issue because it again represents the classic struggle between an individual and a big company. Clients have the continuing belief that they can have whatever they want whenever they want it, even if it means completely disregarding the terms of a prior agreement when it suits their purpose to do so.

I thought I was long past the wrenching battles I fought during my career, but this latest episode again underscores the sobering reality for a songwriter: the only sure protection is in copyright ownership and a fair contract.

I hope that I will not have to rev up again, and go to war again; but I promise that no matter what it takes, the dragon will not win this one.